Advance Praise for "Bridges"

This elegantly written and theologically thoughtful book is so important for these times of chaos and crisis. The Christ you wrote about is not a creedal Christ shut up in a book, but a living Christ whose reconciling action is transforming communities on two continents. Your sacrificial and dedicated discipleship is a humble model of Christ formed leadership. Legendary Black male clergy of different denominations in Dallas, Texas and powerful Black bishops in Nigeria welcomed your leadership as co-minister in community transformation. Your book reminds us that the power of God at work in the beloved community is where there is neither Jew nor Greek, there is neither slave nor free, there is neither male nor female, we all are one in Christ Jesus. It is my prayer that *Bridges: Transforming Communities Together* will bring healing and inspiration to many in our fractured Christian fellowship. This book is an excellent text for emerging leaders.

— Dr. J. Alfred Smith Sr.
Pastor, Allen Temple Baptist Church
Professor Emeritus, Berkeley School of Theology
Author of *On the Jericho Road*

After reading this book, I have concluded that Dr. Kathy Dudley has a God-given passion and gift to turn walls into bridges. I'm driven by the debt that I owe to Kathy and her husband, Sayres, who became members of St Luke "Community" United Methodist Church in Dallas, Texas, where I served as senior pastor for 28 years. It is a predominantly African American congregation that faced and accepted the challenge of serving in a diverse community which led us to put the word "Community" in our name. Indeed with their help, we were able to turn some walls into bridges that remain today. I thank God for her witness, for her family, and all her co-laborers.

— Dr. Zan Wesley Holmes, Jr., Pastor Emeritus
St. Luke "Community" UMC
Author of *When Trouble Comes!*

An elegant and vulnerable autobiography, Dudley traces God's presence in the poverty of her childhood to her calling as a prophet bridge-builder. Beside her husband Sayres, Kathy celebrates God's miraculous leading in their work of reconciliation. Their story is profound and deeply biblical.

> — Dr. Mimi Haddad, President of CBE International
> Co-Author of *Is Women's Equality a Biblical Idea?*

Bridges: Transforming Communities Together is a powerful journey through Kathy Dudley's fascinating life. Her compelling work takes shape, anchored in faith, family, and community. As she navigates complex power structures, and honestly confronts the persistent issues of race and equality she reminds us of what the presence of the Church in the "public square" can and should be. This volume gives a clear voice to the often challenging, but always essential work of authentic partnership in building community. We need this book. We need the bridges that Kathy Dudley, along with so many others, is committed to building.

> — Dr. Derrick Harkins, Director, Center for
> Faith-Based and Neighborhood Partnerships, HUD
> Contributing Author of *The Audacity of Faith*

Dr Kathy Dudley's humble beginnings were just the catalyst God needed to begin a process that would result in nothing short of global transformation. Her steps and missteps along the way are all carefully explained in this book as she leaned into a life of fully trusting God and learned valuable lessons about what it takes to bring about lasting change in even the most desperate of situations. The eventual discovery of the BRIDGE paradigm is Dr. Dudley's gift to a new generation. I highly recommend not just that you read this book but that you incarnate its lessons and be a part of the great things God is doing in the world today.

> — Rev. Keith Stewart, Senior Pastor, Springcreek Church
> Author of *We Were Wrong*

I have had the privilege of traveling to Nigeria with Kathy Dudley twelve times between 2016 and 2020, involved in both the mission outreaches in Badagry and the ILI, teaching pastors the principles of the BRIDGE model. I can testify to the amazing changes during those four years as both Nigerians and Americans grasped the principles of grassroot involvement, taking responsibility for developing ministries, and working together. The principles Kathy puts forth in this book work! I've watched it happen over and over again during the four years of going to Nigeria.

—Dr. Elizabeth "Betsy" Glanville, Senior Affiliate Faculty, Fuller Theological Seminary, School of Mission and Theology

Dr. Kathy Dudley has long been highly regarded for her community development and reconciliation work. In her book, *Bridges*, she reveals the inspiring faith journey and the foundational framework that has guided and sustained her ministry. I encourage you to open the pages of Dudley's book and start building bridges in your community.

—Dr. Curtiss Paul DeYoung, Ed.D.
CEO, Minnesota Council of Churches
Author of *Living Faith: How Faith Inspires Social Justice*

I am honored to call Dr. Kathy both a friend and a pioneer. She has taken on challenges throughout her life. It was my privilege to serve with her during the early years of the development of Voice of Hope. Let me encourage you to read this book and learn more about how God is using Imani Bridges to break down barriers of racism, classism, and sexism. Growing up in Mississippi and having had the privilege of working with Mission Mississippi and encouraging the church to eliminate racism in the body of Christ causes me to celebrate this book and the work of Imani Bridges in an even greater way."

—Dr. Dolphus Weary, Founder, R.E.A.L. Foundation
Author of *I Ain't Comin Back*

Amid the thoughtful responses to inequality in our world, there are few stories I openly celebrate. Both here and abroad, the church can be so tone-deaf and stiff-necked addressing the abusive issues surrounding gender, race, or class. On the other side, the orthodoxy of modern identity politics can be rigid and firmly legalistic. Enter this warm, vulnerable, thoughtful book about how an encounter with Jesus captured the life of a young white sharecropper's daughter from Appalachia and made her a warrior for Christ's Gospel of unity and justice. Kathy Dudley's *Bridges* tells an important story. It is not mere biography; it is witness and testimony about how God shows beauty amid the messiness of life. I celebrate this story as a gift in these confusing times to help us see how to love, be loved, and stand with the people we love.

—Dr. Kwesi R. Kamau, Senior Pastor, Impact Church
Author of *A Better Days* and *A Passion For Prayer*

Bridges: Transforming Communities Together, testifies of Kathy's uncensored obedience to the "heavenly vision" about the BRIDGE paradigm, a relational framework for rallying individuals and groups for collaborative efforts towards achieving societal transformation. The author challenges you to think anew and embrace a new model for missions that is couched in the theology of equality that allows people to contribute from their areas of strength. The book is a dynamic combo showcasing strong intellectual acuity and practical examples seamlessly woven together to demonstrate what God can do when He finds agile leaders like Kathy who are not afraid of stepping into the unknown with no compass but the Holy Spirit alone. I wholeheartedly endorse this book and strongly recommend it as an important text for mission leaders, and all who are involved in transformational ministries across the globe. Enjoy the read and please, share the story.

—Dr. Cosmas Ilechukwu, General Overseer,
Charismatic Renewal Ministries
Author of *The Church Of His Vision*

From Dr. Dudley's upbringing as the daughter of "poor white sharecroppers from the forgotten foothills of southwestern, Virginia" to the national stage of politics and then to being a global influencer of missions and community transformation, her story will challenge you to do and be more. To some of you, I warn you that you may have your theology shaken as Dr. Dudley's love for all people and her tireless efforts with her husband alongside her offended some, but endeared her to many not of her color, culture, or country! Read, be inspired, and be informed.

— Dr. Arthur Gray, Executive Director,
Graysmatters Global Ministries and Consulting

Dr. Dudley's book, *Bridges*, walks the readers through her own personal journey of crossing bridges physically, economically, spiritually, and culturally. She outlines the practical strategies she uses in her ministry and how the BRIDGE framework came about and has been implemented. For those in ministry, this framework centers impacted communities rather than treats them as objects of charity. This book is a great tool as Dr. Dudley invites us to reflect on our journeys and what bridges God may be inviting us to cross.

— Dr. Joyce Del Rosario
Assistant Professor, Pacific School of Religion in Berkley, CA

Born out of a lifetime of service, Dr. Dudley gives us a fresh paradigm for cross-cultural missional engagement. Based on a "theology of equity" this work provides a new approach to serving and partnering with developing world, and domestic, communities in need. This approach is sorely needed as the prior models have created a negative power dynamic which ultimately undermines the often good intentions of those seeking to serve. I would encourage all who desire to serve cross-culturally to read and apply the concepts of this book.

— Rev. John Liotti
CEO / President, Able Works
Board of Directors, CCDA

In this book, Kathy Dudley teaches her readers a framework that when practiced, takes seriously the truth that God is actively at work with each person. Her framework affirms the resources and gifts already present in marginalized persons. When the people's assets are identified, their perspectives are centered, their voices are uplifted, and they are given space to work in collaboration with one another, the people have the power to transform their own communities. Kathy's demonstrated commitment to this model has allowed her and communities she is connected with to see God show up in faith-increasing, powerful, transformative ways, bearing fruit that lasts.

— Bethany Rivera Molinar
Executive Director, Ciudad Nueva Community Outreach
Board Chair, TXCCDN

Kathy Dudley is a prophetic leader committed to a holistic Gospel. Kathy has given her life to the ministry of reconciliation, domestically and internationally. This book illuminates the transformative power of the Gospel of Jesus Christ, illuminating how God took an impoverished child from the Appalachian Mountains who subscribed to a logic of white supremacy and transformed her into an international bridge builder who tirelessly seeks racial, class, and gender reconciliation within a global context. Kathy's life and witness are a gift to the world, and her BRIDGE framework will help the Church faithfully serve as Christ's ambassadors around the world.

— Dominique DuBois Gilliard, Director of Racial Righteousness and
Reconciliation, Evangelical Covenant Church
Author of *Rethinking Incarceration*

For those who want to sit with the hope that God comes to us disguised as our life, I highly recommend this book. It demonstrates the transformative power of believing God is with us and has work for us to do.

— Rev. Rachel Currie Triska
VP of External Affairs, CitySquare

I really enjoyed reading *Bridges: Transforming Communities Together*. Kathy Dudley's book and practical teaching of proven principles are not only effective but also God-breathed. If you're looking for clear teaching with practical examples that can help lead the way to transformational change, born from churches living out God's call to unity, this is the book for you!

— Ava Steaffens, JD, Strategic Partnership
Director for California, World Relief
Past CEO, CCDA

It has been my privilege to watch Dr. Kathy Dudley build bridges for at least a decade and a half. Sitting by kitchen sinks, gathering around leadership palaces, marveling as strong and great leaders, diverse and multiple from all over the world, find a safe space to unpack their gifts and bestow it on others across the face of the earth. I have marveled as one leader, a woman, lead many alpha leaders to the table of communion of minds. I am reading the book . . . I am following the life streams. You should read it too!

— Dr. Oluwasayo Ajiboye
President, RCCGNA Seminary

Dr. Kathy Dudley's life and ministry are the quintessential example of a long obedience in the same direction. In *Bridges*, Dr. Dudley beautifully and transparently articulates, then seamlessly weaves together compelling stories of discovery, identity formation, and radical reconciliation (her own powerful and deeply personal journey notwithstanding). Through an informed and thoughtful application of Biblical texts, theology, and a collaborative, wholistic approach to community transformation, Dudley offers a hope-inspired, time-tested roadmap for how six practical principles, coupled with the power of staying — can lead to beauty and order, unity, and meaningful societal change. This book is a clarion call, to all rooted, socially-motivated, mission-minded practitioners, who are earnestly and faithfully committed to forging authentic, impactful change in the world.

— Rev. Cecilia Williams, President and CEO, CCDA

In this powerful memoir Kathy weaves the core values of her BRIDGE framework with her life story beginning in poverty as the youngest of twelve children born to a sharecropper. She has spent her life empowering people to live better lives. This book gives us a glimpse into her grassroots leadership journey to build bridges in Dallas and Nigeria.

— Dr. Larry Hygh, Jr., Communications Professor
and Public Relations Professional

Bridges: Transforming Communities Together is equal parts riveting story, sound theology and tried and true how-to manual. It is the memoir of a poor, white Virginia sharecropper's daughter moving into a West Dallas neighborhood, then taking the transformation she witnessed to Nigeria. It is a book packed with Biblical teaching from the equity lens of a female theologian. And yet, it is also a doable community development framework proven across two continents.

— Lesa Engelthaler, writer and speaker

I am so thankful for that day when the President of our Mission came into my office and said to me. "Kathy Dudley is coming to see you today. Open your files and your heart to her. God is using her to rescue suffering people. Share with her anything you have that will help her."

That I tried to do. Kathy, thank you on behalf of the healing you helped to facilitate in the communities you touched; thank you for the careers you launched as you treated Black community people with respect, as peers and you encouraged and enabled them to thrive. I thank you on their behalf. My colleague, friend and sister.

— Dr. Willie Peterson, Assistant to the Superintendent,
for the Midsouth Conference of the Evangelical Covenant Church
and Adjunct Professor, Dallas Theological Seminary

In this book, seasoned leader Kathy Dudley pulls the curtain back on what it takes to become a transformative leader. Dudley wears her vital faith on her sleeve and draws from the well of Scripture regularly. Dudley does not shy away from an honest presentation of the joys and challenges of courageous leadership. She has the confidence to follow the vocation God has called her to despite obstacles, but also the humility to learn from others who come from different social locations. With Galatians 3:28 as a particularly strong influence on her understanding of the gospel, Dudley has tackled racism, sexism, and classism head-on to form partnerships that have made communities in various parts of the globe thrive. The spiritual and the practical (education, fresh water, medical care, just economic structures, safe living conditions) are never divorced for Dudley. Her understanding of the gospel of Jesus Christ impels her to invite us all into likewise listening and learning about the needs around us.

— Dr. Jaime Clark-Soles, Professor of New Testament,
Perkins School of Theology, SMU
Author of *Women in the Bible*

Kathy Dudley has written a book that is both inspiring and compelling. It is a compelling narrative that gives encouragement and uplift to the reader. Kathy has tackled Christian Community Development with both a holy boldness and gentle kindness that has been transformational for communities from Dallas to Nigeria. Christian community development begins with people transformed by the love of God, who then respond to God's call to share the Gospel with others through evangelism, social action, economic development, and justice. That is what she has done and continues to do as is explained in this book. She has been my friend since we first met many years ago. After reading her book I understand why we are literally "Soul Sisters!" I highly recommend this as a must read.

— Dr. Lula Bailey Ballton, Director of Community and Economic
Development for the Church of God in Christ International
Author of *Extraordinary Ministry in Ordinary Places*

Kathy Dudley has been a hero and family friend since we first met thirty years ago when I came to be pastor of the church where she and Sayres were members. We were inspired by her vision of biblical equality and Christian community development. More, we were inspired by her commitment to live in and become part of the very community of West Dallas she served. Through the years we have been amazed as God has led her from one field of service to another, from Dallas to Nigeria and beyond, all the while developing and revealing through her the principles through which "God brings people together to heal and build communities through the gospel of Jesus Christ." Through these principles, captured in the model of the BRIDGE, which Kathy has lived out, demonstrated, and proved on the ground so effectively for almost forty years, the entire church can be awakened, equipped, and empowered to become the agent of transformation we are called to be. Her's is an important story and this is a vitally important book.

— Pastor Fred Durham, Director CS Lewis Institute

Without a shred of doubt, my education would have been incomplete if I had not had the privilege of being taught by Dr. Kathy Dudley. I hereby affirm her work and pray that everyone who reads this rare gem of a book will encounter her transformational leadership spirit that has energized me and carried me to many places.

— Pastor Banjo S. Olaniyan, RCCGNA

Bridges

Bridges
Transforming Communities Together

DR. KATHY HODGE DUDLEY

PRECOCITY PRESS

> Due to the wide audience of readers from around the globe in the Imani Bridges network, we have chosen to use American English in this book.

Copyright © 2021 by Kathy Hodge Dudley

All rights reserved. No part of this book may be used or reproduced in any manner without written permission from the author.

Editor: Dr. Sherri Lewis and Dr. Mary Vreugde McCracken
Cover Design and Interior Graphics: Mona Lisa Morris
Creative Director and Designer: Susan Shankin
Precocity Press, Los Angeles, CA

This book contains material protected under International and Federal Copyright Laws and Treaties. No part of this publication may be reproduced, distributed, or transmitted in any form or by any means, including photocopying, recording, or other electronic or mechanical methods, without the prior written permission of the author, except in the case of brief quotations embodied in critical reviews and certain other noncommercial uses permitted by copyright law. For permission requests, email the author at: kathydudley@dudleyandassoc.com

ISBN: 979-8-9851494-1-8
Library of Congress Control Number: 2021921308
First edition printed in the United States of America

All Bible verses are from the TNIV version, unless otherwise noted.

To My Family

I am grateful for being born a Hodge, and I am especially thankful for my parents, James and Hazel Hodge. Being part of a very large family has been an enormous blessing and helped shape my life and values.

I dedicate this book to my lover and life partner, Sayres and my two sons and families: Jonathan, his wife Cara, and two children Aaron and Selah, David, his wife Tricia, and two children Myles and Crystal. This book would not have been possible without you. Desmond Tutu said, "You don't choose your family. They are God's gift to you, as you are to them."

Table of Contents

Forewords	xvii
Introduction	xxiii
Chapter 1. The Journey to Bridge Building	1
Chapter 2. Identity	11
Chapter 3. Purpose	25
Chapter 4. Power	35
Chapter 5. Dallas: Voice of Hope	45
Chapter 6. Texas: Dallas Leadership Foundation	63
Chapter 7. Just Cause	81
Chapter 8. Nigeria and the Birth of Imani Bridges	87
Chapter 9. Phases One and Two of Imani Bridges	95
Chapter 10. Phase Three: Badagry and ILI	109
Chapter 11. Introduction to the BRIDGE™: A Missional Paradigm	127
Chapter 12. The BRIDGE Framework in Scripture	133

Chapter 13. The BRIDGE Framework Principles Part One	141
Chapter 14. The BRIDGE Framework Principles Part Two	151
Chapter 15. Where from Here?	165
Chapter 16. Conclusion	169
Endnotes	173
Acknowlegdments	175
About the Author	177

Forewords

Dr. Ray Bakke
Bakke Graduate University, Past Chancellor
Author of *The Urban Christian* and *A Theology As Big As The City*

Kathy Dudley's story is both authentic and prophetic. The grinding poverty of her childhood gave Kathy an identity she did not need to earn, and instead of defeating her, it motivated her to become an advocate for the disadvantaged. She possesses an emotional intelligence born out of those beginnings, coupled with a whole-hearted commitment to Jesus and an insatiable hunger for the deep truths of God's Word. The BRIDGE framework was birthed in her as a delivery system for holistic Christian ministry, based on a theology of equality, and has now spread from Dallas to Nigeria.

When Kathy entered our global doctoral program, because she lacked previous egress, our academic administrative team was able to give her advanced standing in the light of her amazing accomplishments. Our committee recommended four courses after which we would eliminate the probation and move her to regular status. She so excelled that the academic committee removed her probation after her first two courses.

She pleased me again by inviting my African American friend, Dr. Bill Pannell of Fuller Theological Seminary, to supervise her dissertation. Bill is an exceptional educator and his participation as Kathy's doctoral mentor would guarantee her finished product would match the exceptional work she had already completed throughout our program. We were not disappointed.

The BRIDGE framework, with such a strong biblical foundation is transformative, and is having a true impact in Africa today. This book is both inspiring and enlightening and I highly recommend it.

Dr. William E. Pannell
Professor Emeritus of Preaching, Fuller Seminary
Author of *My Friend, The Enemy* and *The Coming Race Wars*

There is just enough scholar in me that wants to situate this story within the broader context of globalization and the struggle of the church, and churches, to find ways to scratch where suffering people itch. Were I to teach a course in say, evangelism in world turned urban, this would be one of my texts. The Bible would be the main resource since the early evangelists went into all the world and ended up in cities. Many of the early churches, key congregations in the unfolding of the Gospel outreach were urban churches.

We didn't get this information in bible school. I enrolled in one such school upon graduation from high school. I was greener than grass. My early exposure to evangelism and missions was in this setting. Four years later it had become clear that missions were something white Christians did, and that whatever the details were, the action did not require the transformation of the circumstances that ensured that the station in life of their converts should be altered. Converts were to be made but they would remain poor. They would still be the victims of evil forces in high places, still powerless to effect changes that would ensure a better future for their children. Such activism was not on the missionary agenda in those days. This was in the late Forties, early Fifties and evangelicals had yet to discover that much of the world's population was becoming urban. There were movements before then and much more afterward that witnessed world councils meeting to formulate strategies that would effect change in the so-called Third World. The key word was development and the academic components ranged from theology to the social sciences, economics, and global politics.

This book is about Christian mission, and it is a love story. There is theology here and even guidelines for bible studies, but this is also about a young girl who has an encounter with Jesus. This is the story of how this encounter changed her life, redefined her identity and launched a career of remarkable leadership. This is a girl meets boy story which became a partnership in marriage and ministry. Young men beware. This is about a journey from southwest Virginia to Dallas, Texas and from Dallas to Badagry, Nigeria, Africa. Long distances by any map. But then there is an even greater distance from one end of a rickety bridge in Appalachia; one end of which supported a Black community and the other its white counterpart where the only thing these communities had in common was poverty and a mountain spring they both were forced to share. This is a story of how love crossed that bridge and other such structures in Dallas, USA.

But read this story as an exercise in how love dictates changes in strategies that empower people to change their own circumstances. Find yourself being confronted once again by the love of God in Jesus Christ who taught his disciples to love one another and to care for their neighbor. There are strategies involved here of course, but the greatest of these is finding ways to answer the prayer of Jesus that God's children find each other in the warm embrace of love.

Oh, and then there is The Point of Return. This miracle alone is worth the price of the book. Mercy!

Introduction

> "I am where I am because of the bridges that I crossed. Sojourner Truth was a bridge. Harriet Tubman was a bridge. Ida B. Wells was a bridge. Fannie Lou Hamer was a bridge. Madame C.J. Walker was a bridge."
>
> —OPRAH WINFREY

This book is about looking back over the bridges I have crossed to discover how God brings people together to heal and build communities through the Gospel of Jesus Christ. I call it the B.R.I.D.G.E. (BRIDGE) framework.

In this book, we will explore the biblical principles God has given to allow me and others to be a part of centering the church to be an agent of transformation in our world. I share my personal life journey and my theological foundation and core values through the BRIDGE framework. I will expound on my theological beliefs — why and what I believe, and how I have tried to make sense of God and what He is doing in the world.

Sankofa is an Akan term from West Africa that literally means, "to go back and get it." It is symbolized by a mythical bird who has its feet firmly planted forward, but its head turned backwards. Practically, the concept means that in every aspect of life — artistic, spiritual, business, etc. — you cannot move forward until you've looked back and absorbed where you've been. There is much wisdom to be found in this analogy.

In 1996, while I was president of Dallas Leadership Foundation (DLF), the Lord woke me in the middle of the night and revealed the BRIDGE framework (figure 1). The "BRIDGE" is an acronym for belief, relationship, interdependence, development, grassroots-driven, and empowerment.

It represents the principles and theological belief system I had informally practiced for many years while ministering to the homeless and then

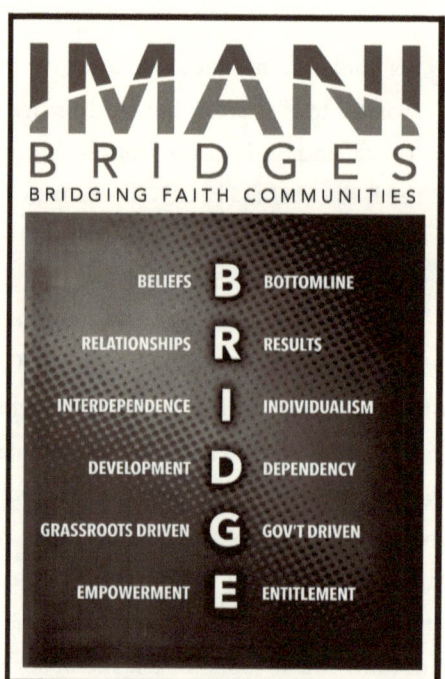

Figure 1

at Voice of Hope, a ministry I founded with my husband in 1982. However, DLF provided a perfect playground to be intentional about using this framework.

In the diagram above, the new paradigm principles are on the left side of the word, BRIDGE. In contrast, on the right side are the modes of operation commonly used in general society. To embrace the new paradigm does not necessarily mean the principles on the right are not valuable. It is simply how they are emphasized.

It is my belief that the principles on the left, when laid on a foundation of biblical equality, far exceed those on the right in bringing fruitfulness and transformational change to the individual, church, and society. This is partly because the belief system on the left provides for full participation and a sense of "ownership" of the vision from those historically disenfranchised and marginalized in our society.

People and groups will not lose their voice when uniting under these principles. In fact, the more marginalized they are, the more their voice will be able to increase, because of the aim to balance the scales of equality. We have used these principles to guide the decisions and commitments of DLF and Imani Bridges, the organization I founded in 2004 with several African bishops.

In Nigeria, the benefit of having so many great African leaders agree to focus on utilizing the BRIDGE as a framework for societal transformation has helped to mature the understanding of just how powerful it is. This framework has provided a common belief system and language to facilitate collaborative action, and created a platform for God to do the unimaginable and miraculous.

This book is the telling of my story, but also of countless others who have decided to embrace the use of the BRIDGE framework. Throughout the book, you will find voices of both American and Nigerian partners in transformation. You will be able to hear them speak in their own words about what the BRIDGE means to them, and how they have utilized it.

It is my prayer that you will find these stories inspiring and principles helpful as you seek to find new tools to assist you on your journey.

I do not feel qualified to say I recommend this book. I feel drawn to tell the world, rather, that I have gone into a learning mode, to be taught by a Master Teacher, using this tool, the book in my hand. This book is not theoretical, it is forged in powerful relationships. These relationships are not on the surface; they are deep wells: they are linked in the quiet place, far away from the noise of the cityscape. This book is not just about the thoughts of one person, it is about the distilled lives of multiple leaders; leaders to whom this one person consciously reached out and impacted: in the name of Jesus.

– Dr. Oluwasayo Ajiboye, President, RCCGNA Seminary

CHAPTER 1

The Journey to Bridge Building

It was Sunday night, March 26, 2017. Our tired and dedicated team of seventeen Americans from Imani Bridges, who had just ministered all week were at the Lagos airport in Nigeria, preparing for the eighteen-hour journey home. Nigerian sisters and brothers were also journeying home in cars and vans to twenty different parts of the country, some up to thirteen hours away. Our local Badagry volunteers were settling into their homes after an extraordinary week of fruitful ministry in the intense heat of the equatorial climate.

Then God showed up, as only God can.

What happened?

Mission trips involving Americans take place across the globe every month and have for decades. What was so unusual about this week in Badagry? One must first understand the setting to comprehend the significance of what happened.

Badagry, Nigeria is a port city with both a famous and infamous history. The first missionaries to Nigeria landed there in 1841, yet for centuries, hundreds of thousands of enslaved Africans had been forced onto ships at Badagry's Point of No Return. The first church, hospital and school in Nigeria were established in Badagry in the ensuing years ... nonetheless, Nigerians considered it cursed for generations, due to the transatlantic slave trade. While the message of the Christian Gospel spread inland into West Africa, countless men, women, and children were marched in chains to Badagry, destined for lands unknown.

From 2004–2017, I made numerous visits to Badagry with Nigerian church leaders and pastors from various denominational backgrounds, with whom God had brought me into relationship. We visited the cells where the enslaved were held in inhuman conditions for weeks or even months. We then traveled the short distance together to The Point of No Return on the Atlantic Ocean beach where the enslaved were loaded into boats and taken to the ships for the long and often deadly journey, the Middle Passage.

In March of 2017, we had our second, week-long outreach in Badagry. Seventeen racially diverse, American team members traveled from various locales to join 356 volunteers from across Nigeria. One hundred nine of the Nigerians represented local Badagry churches. The remaining Nigerians, also from various tribes and denominations — Catholic to Pentecostal — traveled up to thirteen hours to participate.

As the week began without any fanfare, some of the pastors gathered at various places throughout the city to pray that God would destroy the hold of the enemy on the city. One of the shrines where they prayed was a 250-year-old Iroko tree near City Hall — where various kinds of sacrifices had been made for centuries.

The forecast had been hot and rainy, but we saw no rain the entire week, the smallest of miracles. Throughout the week, ministry took place across the city. Fifteen tracks of vocational training occurred simultaneously, mostly taught by Nigerians. Medical clinics staffed with Nigerian doctors and nurses saw thousands of patients. Adult and child evangelism teams went throughout the city, including to schools that opened their doors for teams to come and share the Gospel with the children. Evangelistic meetings were held each evening by local churches with Imani Bridges banners clearly displayed. For this week, the churches worked as one under the banner of Imani Bridges.

On Thursday afternoon, we paused for a few hours from these important activities. A group of local Nigerians and national Nigerian Christian leaders and members joined the American team on a small, yet significant pilgrimage to remember and experience what the enslaved had experienced — a crushing sense of despair. The cramped, dark, stifling cells where West Africans were imprisoned, waiting to be sold to the next ship of European slave traders, was an overwhelming and nightmarish experience.

The conditions were inhuman. Many of the enslaved did not survive the cells. Our tears flowed freely. It was a sobering and very personal experience, especially for the African American members of our team. Our Nigerian partners, godly men and women, shared this time of deep reflection.

From there, we walked across the road to a small lagoon and boarded boats, probably similar in size to what the enslaved would have been forced into, though we were not in their chains. After crossing the lagoon, we walked the last sweltering mile through sand to the ocean. Our last stop before the beach was a well where the enslaved were forced to drink and were told they would now forget their entire identity. With their identity stripped, and chains binding them, they were forced onto ships.

This journey, at this place, was taken by approximately 30% of all the enslaved who were shipped out of West Africa.[1] As the enslaved looked back from aboard the ship to the city that had betrayed them, they undoubtedly cursed Badagry where many locals had partnered in this horrific trade.

During this week in 2017, and on this pilgrimage to The Point of No Return, the identity of the city and beach were being transformed. The Nigerian church leaders decided this place was so significant, they wanted to change the name. They repented on behalf of their ancestors and asked forgiveness of their African American brethren, who had now become friends. We circled and held hands, and Rev. Peter Egho, the Nigeria Director for Imani Bridges, led us in prayer and renamed that place, The Point of Return.

Nigerian and American teams join hands to pray and announce the renaming the infamous beach to *The Point of Return*.

It was a sacred moment and moved us all to tears. Built upon the prayers of the pastors earlier in the week throughout the city, and the prayers of repentance and declaration at the beach, the Nigerian church leaders reclaimed the beach for God's glory, declaring it The Point of Return. There was a miracle of identity breakthrough, and the releasing of the curse on the land.

The breaking of the curse was confirmed on Sunday. After the non-local Nigerians had left Badagry, and the Americans awaited their flight home, miles away in Lagos, God struck the Iroko tree in the city, near City Hall, with fire from above. There was no observable reason the tree should have caught fire in the middle of the trunk.

When the fire department attempted to put out the fire with water and flame-suppressing chemicals, the flames actually exploded and grew, spreading up the tree. They emptied three fire trucks to no avail, and eventually focused on simply protecting the surrounding buildings as charred branches fell harmlessly to the ground. About seventeen hours later, the fire burned itself out, leaving those on the ground to realize that miraculously, only the tree had burned, but not the leaves of an unrelated vine that wound around the tree.²

Those vines had not been a part of the original tree. Truly, God had worked a miracle. However, there could not have been this Sunday of breakthrough without the Thursday of prayer and healing that happened just days before at what we now called The Point of Return.

The transformation of identity was further confirmed about a month later when we were alerted that Lagos State had officially, with no connection to us, renamed the beach in Badagry — previously called The Point of No Return — The Point of Return.

The Iroko tree, for years the site of sacrifices in the middle of Badagry, after the "unquenchable fire." Notice the non-indigenous leaves did not burn.

When I later talked with the Nigerian church leaders that I had been in fellowship with for over thirteen years, I encouraged them that this event could be likened to the baptism of Jesus. God who became Man, was baptized by John the Baptist. God the Holy Spirit landed on the Son's shoulder, and God the Father spoke from heaven about Jesus' identity. God said, "This is my Son, whom I love; with him I am well pleased." (Matthew 3:17).

I told our Nigerian pastors that what happened this week in Badagry was God saying, "This is my beloved Church with whom I am well pleased." I stood in awe of how far we'd come, and all that God had done.

A new belief system with strong biblical foundation must replace the belief system that stems from the African Traditional Religion (ATR), which essentially controls the thinking and actions of many Africans today. The ATR bequeathed Africans with the belief system that is driven by fear of the spirits, divinities, and ancestors.

However, the BRIDGE paradigm espouses a faith-driven belief system founded on the teachings of the Bible and awash with the overflowing love of God for His creation. God is the Supreme Spirit and exercises unbridled sovereignty over every other being, spiritual or mundane. As Africans begin to understand that this Supreme Spirit is their Father and that He has conferred on them all the privileges of children, then a new vibrant faith will be birthed in the people.

– Dr. Cosmas Ilechukwu, General Overseer,
Charismatic Renewal Ministries

Getting There

How did I, a poor, white sharecropper's daughter from the forgotten foothills of southwestern Virginia, come to be a part of bringing transformation through unity and the reformation of identities in Badagry, Nigeria?

My entire childhood unfolded in a rural community called Barren Springs, where like most communities in the late 1950s and 1960s, it was racially divided and segregated. A swinging bridge swayed high above a creek that spanned our divide. Some rungs were missing, and it was not an easy bridge to cross. Only one Black family and the community's Black church were on our side of that bridge among the white folk — the same side where the freshwater spring was. All the other Black families lived on the other side and had to cross the rickety bridge to get their water.

From my isolated environment, God led me to college, and eventually, with my husband Sayres, to Dallas, Texas. In Dallas, I started two organizations: Voice of Hope (VOH) in 1982, and later, Dallas Leadership Foundation (DLF) in 1995. These two organizations were started out of a desire to bring societal transformation in some of the poorest areas of Dallas. Through our years in Dallas, the principles of the BRIDGE framework emerged.

In 2004, I was surprised to be asked to share what I had learned in Dallas with a class of seventeen bishops in Nigeria. I was even more surprised that from that class emerged a fellowship of leaders who wanted me to help them learn to grow in unity and ultimately implement the BRIDGE framework in their contexts. They wanted to work together to see church-centered societal transformation.

From this desire, Imani Bridges was born. "Imani" means "faith" in Swahili. We wanted to build faith bridges. Now, at the time of writing this book in 2021, we are encouraged to see the beginnings of societal transformation taking root in the country of Nigeria.

I didn't know it as a child, but even early on, God was laying the foundation in my heart for an understanding of how to build bridges that would lead to societal transformation:

- bridges between white and people of color, rich and poor, male and female, young and old, and any other perceived inequalities found in our world
- bridges that empower people to find their identity, purpose, and power
- bridges that bring unity and societal transformation

My identity began taking shape in a tiny, impoverished Virginia hamlet, as the twelfth child of poor, white sharecroppers. However, through my journey, God has led me to a place of identity in Him, given me purpose in His Kingdom, and blessed me to be an agent of transformation. This is the story of my journey.

I've learned how to build bridges that help to bring this transformation — bridges that connect, draw out identity, give purpose, and empower. My book is full of stories and the principles I believe God revealed to me along the way — principles that can be applied both individually and systemically.

In June of 2005, I had just finished writing my dissertation that covered the BRIDGE framework and my journey to that point. It was printed out and sitting on my home office desk when Peter Egho, a Nigerian bishop, and his wife, Diana, arrived at our house in California. It was Diana's first trip to the U.S., and my first time meeting her.

The next morning, I woke up and went into my office. I was surprised to find Diana sitting at my desk. She hadn't been able to sleep and had spent the whole night reading. I stumbled upon her just as she finished my entire dissertation. As soon as she saw me, she stood up, extremely excited. She pointed to my dissertation and said, "*This* is Africa! *This* is Africa!"

Once more, very recently, a successful, African American businesswoman came into our Imani Bridges office in Dallas and saw a picture of

Dr. Bill Pannell and Rev. Peter and Diana Egho, celebrating my graduation from Bakke Graduate University, at our home in Pasadena, CA in 2005.

the BRIDGE framework on the wall. After reading and absorbing it, she exclaimed, "This should be everywhere!" She could see her story and our story, and how they fit together.

My hope is that you will not just see my journey, or even our journey at Imani Bridges, but that you will find *your* journey in these reflections as well. As others already have, be inspired to continue moving forward in bringing transformation to the communities around you.

Dr. Kathy's contribution to the Nigerian church and leaders is a case study. She's one of the very few who has broken protocols. The anointing to bring churches and leaders together to pursue a common cause could only be from God. One of the things I have learned from IB is that everyone has a contribution to make. Also, we give people more value when we get them to contribute whatever they can to get the work done. There's strength in unity, and we leverage every potential that God has put in people.

—Bishop Sam Airiohuodion
General Overseer, House of Levites Chapel International

CHAPTER 2

Identity

Brothers and sisters, think of what you were when you were called. Not many of you were wise by human standards; not many were influential; not many were of noble birth. But God chose the foolish things of the world to shame the wise; God chose the weak things of the world to shame the strong. God chose the lowly things of this world and the despised things — and the things that are not — to nullify the things that are, so that no one may boast before him. It is because of him that you are in Christ Jesus, who has become for us wisdom from God — that is, our righteousness, holiness, and redemption. Therefore, as it is written: "Let the one who boasts boast in the Lord."

1 Corinthians 1: 26-31

Identity plays a large role in transformation, both at the individual and the community level. A lot of what I learned about how to be an instrument of transformation was because of what I experienced in my upbringing.

My Dad, James Hodge, holding me as a baby.

SHAPED IN POVERTY

Poverty was inbred into our family for generations. Growing up in the Appalachian Mountains, I came to know poverty's devastating effects firsthand. The southwest part of Virginia was an area where the poor — both Black and white — experienced generational poverty. My identity was interwoven with this and was something I continually struggled with for years.

When I started school in first grade, my awareness of our poverty became acute. In the spring, summer, and fall, we could pretty much get away with not having our extreme poverty exposed. However, come winter, when the cold winds and rain blew against rickety wooden houses, those who were extremely poor had to board up their windows. There were so many broken panes in our house that without covering them up, we would freeze. When the school bus arrived, the children on the bus would jeer and

This is me at about 4 years old. I was a very shy and insecure little girl.

ridicule me when they saw the windows covered with paper. Suddenly, my identity as a very poor child was exposed.

We had no running water and had to haul it from the spring. Water was precious and scarce. We caught the rainwater for washing clothes and feeding the animals. This left little water for bathing, cooking, and drinking. In other words, we were dirty most of the time.

When I attended first grade, the teacher decided to teach us a lesson about personal cleanliness. She inspected each of our hands and knees for dirt. If they were dirty, she took a ruler and hit our outstretched hands. You can imagine the self-image this ingrained in me, and how I felt when she hit me. In my feeble attempts to clean myself, I would spit on my hands on the way to school to try and get the dirt off to avoid this disgrace.

The home I grew up in, taken in 2007. It was already in ruin.

Even Christmas became a time of reinforcing my low self-esteem. At age nine, my mother took me to a charity where they were giving out Christmas presents to the children. Mom told me I would receive a doll. We stood in line while people across the street pointed and jeered at us. I felt terrified and exposed. Finally, when they got to us at the end of the line, they handed me the doll. It was naked and dirty, and I thought, *Well, this looks just like me. This is what I deserve.*

Besides broken windows, the plaster walls inside the house were full of holes; big ones, with mice running up and down the walls. My oldest brother was once bitten by a mouse. I was constantly afraid.

Our poverty glared at me again every time my sister and I had to retrieve water in a huge, five-gallon jug by dipping it into the spring. It was so heavy, every few steps we would change hands to carry it the half-mile up the hill back to our home. To this day, I credit my arm strength to hauling that water.

I was naturally very athletic. Coaches and teachers at school regularly asked me to play sports or be on various teams. However, I could not because my parents did not have a car, and we lived seventeen miles from school. In all these things, I knew I was different. Even if I was strong or gifted, there was no opportunity for me do things others seemed to be doing.

Education held little value in my home. My mother had a fourth-grade education, and my dad was illiterate. I had no one to help me with my schoolwork, and family expectations were different.

A defining moment occurred when I was entering high school. One of my older sisters told me, "Soon it will be time for you to quit school and go to work." She was preparing me for the only inevitable future she saw for me. Graduating from high school was not a family value.

When I responded that I had no plans to work in the factory, the reaction was strong. The clan dynamics began with questions like, "Do you think you're better than us?" "Everybody up to you has had to do that, so why do you think you're different?" These incidences continually ate at me from within and without and made it very difficult to climb out of poverty.

All of this and more contributed to my understanding the challenges facing me if I chose to be different. I no longer would have the understanding of my family. Escaping a poverty identity is first a mental battle — how do you see yourself and how do others see you?

Part of my mental battle was fighting for beauty and order in a system that did not encourage it. There was no garbage collection service in our area. What did we do with cans, cartons, old clothes, and anything else that accumulated that was no longer useful? Our solution was to throw it all over the fence where the cows would then come and scatter it across the big field.

I remember as a little girl, wanting beauty so much, and knowing something was wrong with what we were doing. So, I climbed over the fence and made piles of the trash. No sooner would I finish, the cows would kick and spread it around again. My next plan was to figure how to get some of it into grocery bags and then take it down the road and throw it over the riverbank. That is what I did.

It was so difficult to not lose hope. When does one just give up and say, "I can't do anything about this? This is my lot in life, so I'll just throw the trash over the fence and not worry about it?"

My Parents

My father, James Hodge, was a hard worker. When I was young, he worked on the farm that surrounded our small homestead, purchased sacrificially

My Mom and Dad, Hazel and James Hodge.
I love you so much.

by my oldest sister when she began working as a teenager. As the eldest son of eleven children, he had attended school for a few months before leaving to assist in raising his other siblings.

I was always drawn to my father because of his extreme talent and intelligence. He played numerous musical instruments, and my heart would fill with joy at the sound of his playing the banjo, fiddle, or guitar. Sometimes all he had to do was pick up a set of spoons; he could even make spoons sing!

There was no end to his creativity. One day, I watched him gather several pieces of junk, lay them on the kitchen table, and explain how he would create a lamp. To my amazement, he proceeded to do exactly that. I was thrilled and proud to see the lamp light burning. Beyond his talent and intellect, however, I was most drawn to his warmth and affection. Sitting on his lap and cuddled in his arms, I felt secure and deeply loved. As I grew older, I became perplexed at the dichotomy. Why was this man who possessed such talent, so poor?

By my fourth birthday, my father suffered from several sunstrokes and lost his ability to work. In the next years, he sank into deep despair. He hung his fiddle on the wall and refused to play any other instruments. Though not yet fifty, he could no longer care for his family. He didn't know how to handle the embarrassment and accusations, so he turned to drinking. Unable to afford wine or liquor, he often drank rubbing alcohol to ease his pain.

When he wasn't drinking, he was gentle, sweet, and unbelievably kind, but when he was drunk, he changed into a mean and dangerous man. Catherine Meeks wrote "a person without hope is dangerous."[3] I saw with my own eyes how true this was for my father. The alcohol made him truly crazy, and the loving, wonderful man whom I adored, and who adored me, was now chasing us out of the house, waving a gun and shouting obscenities.

My mom, my sister, Alice, and I would run down the little dirt road to hide in the bushes until he finally passed out. One time, my mom did not make it to safety and Dad hit her with a wine bottle across her face and

Mom, Dad, my sisters Sylvia and Alice, and me in Dad's arms.

broke her nose. It bled profusely. I remember Mom never defined Dad by that period of his life; she just loved him unconditionally.

Hazel Hodge, my mother, was a very special, God-fearing woman. She may have been simple, but she loved God and loved her family. I will always remember her singing hymns as she worked around the house. Her presence and her influence were felt even as she lay dying. She sang her favorite hymns with her eight remaining children, twenty plus grandchildren, and numerous great grandchildren surrounding her bed in the little,

IDENTITY • 19

Even when I was a teenager, I loved to snuggle with my Daddy.

two-room house. Several of our family members committed their lives to Christ because of the way she lived and witnessed to God's love in those last moments.

Hope

I tried to fight a poverty mentality the best I knew how. At age fifteen, I was selected to go to Virginia Polytechnic Institute in Blacksburg, Virginia for Upward Bound. Upward Bound was a two-summer program designed to help underprivileged teenagers (the poorest kids at the school) attend college.

In the second summer before my senior year of high school, at the lowest point in my life, I arrived on campus and met my roommate, Diane. I was hurting and desperately in need of someone with whom to discuss my troubles. She told me she was a Christian and committed to pray for my father each day, that he would stop drinking.

She also spent the summer secretly hand-making a beautiful, new, pink dress for me with her small stipend and extra time. I was surprised with her gift just before we left for home.

I was, and still am amazed that this young, poor, sixteen-year-old girl cared so much for me. I realize now it was the love of God in her that reached out to me tangibly in my time of crisis.

Arriving home, I was shocked to find Diane's prayers answered. My father was sober with a fresh commitment to remain that way. He only relapsed a few times before dying five years later. Here was God, paving the way even before I knew Him.

Though I had yet to surrender to Him, God was reframing the way I thought. I had a new confidence and was discovering how to help others in this process. I decided to start the Upward Bound Club, the first of its kind in our high school. It was an upside-down model.

Previously, teenagers had been ashamed to be associated with Upward Bound, because it was where all the poor kids went. However, in the club I started, everyone could join, but only poor kids could be officers. Wealthier kids joined the club as well. They participated in listening to speakers, and writing articles for our school paper about education and our experiences visiting universities and colleges. I was discovering the ability to change the way I thought and to create new ways for others to think differently as well.

Racism

Racism was another issue in my life journey. I absorbed racial prejudice as part of my upbringing. Our tiny, racially divided hamlet gave me my first exposure to African Americans. About once a month, the Black community had church services in their building on our side of the creek. Instinctively, I would take a pail of water and a dipper to offer a drink to those passing as they walked to church. Afterwards, I would get scolded by my siblings because our dipper now "had" to be sterilized.

Sometimes, we were very mischievous children. My sister and I would wait until everyone was inside the church. Then we would scurry to hear the beautiful music, and peep in the windows to distract and irritate the congregation. Josie Miller, the Black lady who lived next to the church and served as church caretaker, was especially annoyed with us. On other days, we ran into her yard to steal apples off her tree, only to find ourselves running from the sound of a gun.

In my first summer in the Upward Bound program, I was assigned a room with an African American girl. Because of my inbred racial prejudice, I rejected this arrangement and requested a new roommate. My request was denied, but we eventually were separated because of how tense our situation grew.

My racist attitude possibly devastated this young girl. My response to her didn't make any sense. We were both extremely poor and recipients of the same government program, but I considered myself superior.

Identity Transformation

During the summer of 1971, after my junior year in high school, I convinced the welfare department in a nearby town to let me work there. I was hired again in the summer of 1972 before attending college. That summer, God divinely intervened when the superintendent decided to hire two of us. The other student was a Christian. Two weeks before going to college, I followed her to a youth camp meeting and gave my life to Jesus Christ.

During my first week at Ferrum College, an African American girl accused me of being a racist because of a comment I made in class. Instead of reacting or making the situation worse as I would have before, I pulled her aside after class and asked her to help me understand what I had said that offended her. She was shocked by my response, but agreed to talk to me. We later became close friends.

As I pondered this event years later, I was amazed at the difference in my reaction to these two girls. In only a few short weeks, the Lord began to transform my attitude about people who were different from me. As a Christian, I now knew I was not superior to people of color and that God created us all as equals. As I studied the Scriptures, God showed me Galatians 3:28, "There is neither Jew nor Gentile, neither slave nor free, neither male nor female, for you are all one in Christ Jesus." This Scripture became a pillar of truth in my life.

Christianity was not entirely new to me because of my mother's spiritual influence in my life. However, I saw her religion and faith as too simplistic, and undesirable. Unlike dad, my mom had a difficult time showing affection, and felt she showed her love best by serving, not talking. It would be many years before I learned to appreciate my mother's incredible faith and steadfastness. I can still hear her singing "Amazing Grace" early in the morning, as she built the fire in the wood cook-stove and prepared breakfast.

As a young Christian of seventeen, long before I came to appreciate my mother's faith, I began to realize the wisdom and lifechanging power in the Scriptures. The Lord began to work in my life. I ate God's Word like bread and was hungry for a relationship with my newfound Savior and Friend. Instinctively, I knew He had the answers to my questions and would give me a sense of purpose and hope. This new faith allowed me to look at my poverty, parents, and future through a different life lens.

Through my study of the Scriptures, I learned what it meant to be "in Christ," and to have Christ live in me. The only way I could say "no" to my human desires was to deepen my "yes" to Christ, which meant I must also say "yes" to my self-identity and worth. The more I faced this reality, the more genuinely I turned to Christ.

Through this understanding of who I was in Christ, I avoided being hampered and paralyzed by the many painful memories and the unresolved conflicts in my family and community.

I could now find my identity not only in my earthly parents, but also in my heavenly Parent. Christ was all I needed. I could discover who I really was in Him. I died, and my new life was found hidden in Christ (Col. 3:3).

I was Kathy, daughter of James and Hazel Hodge, but I was also Kathy, child of God. This revelation helped me understand more fully what the Apostle Paul meant in Galatians 2:20, "I have been crucified with Christ and I no longer live, but Christ lives in me. The life that I now live in the body, I live by faith in the son of God, who loved me and gave himself for me."

I could also understand Paul's struggle in Romans 7, and his victorious proclamation: "Therefore, there is now no condemnation for those who are in Christ Jesus, because through Christ Jesus the law of the Spirit who gives life has set you free from the law of sin and death" (Rom. 8:1).

Like Peter, I proclaimed, "You are the Christ, the son of the living God" (Matt. 16:16). Little by little, the Lord was making me a new creation for His glory and purpose. I was beginning to learn that equality in Christ and finding my identity in Christ were foundational to transformation.

CHAPTER 3

Purpose

My new identity began to give me purpose and the desire to bring hope and transformation to others. Almost immediately, I sensed God's call on my life to help others. It wasn't long before God brought along someone wonderful to partner with me in this calling.

A popular song of the 1960s by Billy Joe Royal was "Down in the Boondocks." In the song, Billy Joe talks about being put down because he grew up in the boondocks. Coincidently, the place I grew up was nicknamed, "Boon." The song continues though, saying, "Some fine day, I'll find a way to move from this old shack. Hold my head up like a king and never ever look back." I memorized this song because it described exactly how I felt. My dream was to get an education, get out of poverty, leave Barren Springs, and never look back.

Sayres

I met Sayres Dudley not long after arriving at college. We attended a Bible study and started dating soon after. Several weeks later, I was praying and asked the Lord, "Is Sayres the one You have chosen for me?"

I felt like I heard the Lord say, "He will part, he will return, and you will marry." Shortly after, Sayres came to me and said, "I believe God is saying we are not to date." I was crushed, but not really surprised.

Regularly, the members of our Christian fellowship would travel a couple of hours to Clifton Forge, Virginia to a small home fellowship and spend the weekend there. Shirley Bruffey was an amazing woman and great leader. Most of us saw her as our spiritual mother. I decided I would tell her what I believed the Lord had told me about Sayres.

She strongly advised me to not mention this to anyone. She said, "You will never know for sure if this was God speaking if you share it with others. Ponder it in your heart, and if this is from God, it will come to pass."

For six and a half months we didn't date but stayed in fellowship. In the spring semester, we even found ourselves sitting across from one another in our Sociology class, Marriage and the Family. During that class, I secretly wrote our wedding ceremony for a class project.

On April 12, 1973, a young woman visited me on campus and shared a word she felt the Lord had given her for me. She said, "I know that the Lord spoke to you about marriage and who the person is. The Lord is moving. Also, you will get married soon and that person is Sayres Dudley."

I couldn't believe my ears. I had told no one other than Shirley. I had pondered this in my heart and prayed that God's will would be done. Now it seemed that God was confirming His word and I decided to wait with expectation.

On April 27th, several Christians on campus decided to go to Roanoke to hear Paul Stookey, of Peter, Paul and Mary fame. To my surprise, Sayres asked if I wanted to ride with him. I said yes, and along with another couple, we were on our way. It was a small group at the Hotel Roanoke, sitting in a circle with Stookey in the middle of the room on a small stool. After a few songs, he started to sing "The Wedding Song." This was the main song I had put in the wedding ceremony I had written for class.

Sayres and I were sitting next to one another and when I heard the song, I asked God, "If it was really You that spoke to me, would You have Sayres take my hand?"

Suddenly, Sayres reached over and grabbed my hand. I thought my heart was going to jump out of my chest.

On the way back to campus, I sat close to Sayres in the car with my head on his shoulder. I decided to ask God for a confirmation again. "Lord, if You really did speak to me, please have Sayres start singing 'The Wedding Song.'" Immediately, Sayres began to sing the song. During this same time, Sayres was also having a conversation with the Lord. He will now share what happened in his own words.

We were all so excited to drive forty miles to hear a famous artist like Paul Stookey and were surprised upon arrival at a room in the Hotel Roanoke to learn how small the crowd was. Kathy sat on the floor next to me and I began having some romantic feelings. When Stookey sang his famous song, I reached out and held Kathy's hand for the first time in almost seven months. The rest of the evening was wonderful, but when the concert was over, we hustled out to the car, because all Ferrum girls had a midnight curfew and it was 11 pm.

With her in the front seat, I drove quickly back to campus. I loved singing, so I began to quietly sing "The Wedding Song," and my heart was filled with joy at this moment. The car was quiet and as I began to meditate on God's goodness, a conversation began in my head and I sensed God speaking to me. It went something like this.

"You really enjoyed tonight, didn't you?"

"Yes Lord, it was great."

"You liked being with Kathy Hodge again, didn't you?"

"Oh yes, Lord, very much!"

"I brought you together and she is going to be your wife."

"What did You say, Lord??"

"Kathy is going to be your wife."

"But Lord, how can this be?"

"Not only is she going to be your wife, but you will ask her to marry you tonight."

For the remaining trip, I was in this surreal conversation with God, but as I drove, the peace of God rested on me, and by the time we reached campus, I knew this was right.

We raced into the parking lot of her dorm at 12:02 pm, and the stern dorm mother was standing at the door, arms crossed, and girls were jumping out of cars and rushing in. I told the other couple to get out and as Kathy began to move towards the door, I stopped her.

With no time to figure out the right words, I blurted out, "Kathy, if it is God's will, will you marry me?"

She screamed, "YES," threw her arms around me, jumped out of the car, and ran to the dorm.

I was left alone in the car with the realization of what just happened, scared but excited, knowing God had spoken.

Divided by Class

Sayres grew up in Middleburg, Virginia, which was an elitist small town. President Kennedy and his family had a home there in the 1960s, and it wasn't uncommon to see Jackie Kennedy and the kids walking down the street. Elizabeth Taylor even owned a mansion in the town. Pristine lawns and storybook houses dotted the verdant landscape. The famous Red Fox Inn was a symbol of the rich history and culture that permeated the entire area for generations.

Though the Dudley's had lost much of their wealth by this time, there remained the legacy of a rich history. Sayres' grandfather was a president of Middleburg National Bank, and his father had served as a judge and attorney in nearby Leesburg. Even as the large Dudley estate was in disrepair, its old Virginia colonial house was a reminder of an impenetrable class structure that separated people like Sayres and me.

While celebrating Sayres' graduation from Ferrum with his parents in May 1973, we announced our marriage plans. Mr. and Mrs. Dudley were

Our wedding in November 1973, with Mom and Dad.
My father would pass away less than 2 years later.

in utter shock. It was difficult for them to accept that their son was going to marry a poor farmer's daughter from southwest Virginia. How could this have happened?

Earlier in the year, Sayres had been drafted into the Army, but to finish the year in college, he had agreed to serve a six-year term in the Air Force upon graduation. In November 1973, just after Sayres finished boot camp, training, and celebrated his twenty-first birthday, we were married. I was nineteen years old. Our marriage meant I had to drop out of college, but there was no doubt this was God's plan for my life. With no money for a honeymoon, we left Virginia immediately and headed north to Massachusetts for his first tour of duty. This girl from "down in the boondocks" was about to experience a whole new world.

A kiss to begin our lifelong adventure and love affair.

Equality in Marriage

Equality was tested early in our marriage. Sayres did not grow up with any sisters and had no idea how to do day-to-day life with a woman. The first time we went grocery shopping together was in the military commissary. It had one entrance, and a one-way path through the store, leading to the checkout stand. You only had one chance to pick up any item. As we began walking through, I chose some things and put them in the basket. Sayres looked at my choices, silently decided we didn't need them, and promptly put them back on the shelves.

I tolerated this for about two or three items, until he was about to put a jar of maraschino cherries back on the shelf. I couldn't hold it in any longer. Right there, in the middle of the store, I stopped the buggy, with everyone in the store now looking at us and said, "If it's going to be this way, I'm going to go get a job, and make my own money."

That got his attention, because we had agreed that I would donate my time to the church and to ministry. I was asserting that if we had made that decision together, I would not be controlled or have my decisions taken away from me as to whether I wanted a Coke or maraschino cherries.

To this day, we keep a jar of maraschino cherries in our refrigerator as a reminder and a symbol of the equality we stand for together. Sayres will tell you he had been swimming in male privilege and was not even aware of his actions or how he was behaving. So, when I said, "No," that day in the store, he began asking himself why he had even been trying to control my decisions. He immediately saw how ridiculous it was.

And that has been the beauty of Sayres throughout our marriage. Though born into privilege as a well-to-do white man, he did not personally encounter the sting of racism, classism, or sexism, but he has not been afraid to learn and to change.

Finding Purpose in New England

One of the most difficult adjustments we made in moving to Massachusetts was the weather. It seemed winter would never end. Once the snow began, it was months before it melted and the sun returned. People were different also — more direct and less friendly, but also honest. I learned to value this over the next five years.

After five months of marriage, we decided to start a family, and I quickly became pregnant. I was also pregnant with the need to reach out and share my newfound faith with others. We decided to initiate an outreach to single, Air Force men living in the dormitories on base. This was strategic, because shortly after our arrival at Westover Air Force Base, officials decided to close the base, leaving only one all-male unit remaining. Many married families like ours had to live off base. We saw this as a great opportunity to witness to the isolated single men about the love of God. Little by little, some of the airmen began to respond.

Simultaneously, our hearts were burdened to sponsor an orphan overseas, but with nothing left over each month after tithe and bills, this was difficult to do. Apple pie evangelism was born out of this dual burden. Combining and modifying recipes from several of our friends, the Lord taught me how to make a delicious pie from apples we gathered from a local orchard.

An idea developed. Sell the pies to airmen on base, and the money earned would allow us to support a child. When the men arrived at our apartment Thursday night to pick up the pies, we strategically planned a home Bible study. We invited them to stay for our meeting and enjoy apple pie for dessert. After, they would take their own whole pie home to enjoy later. The strategy worked and many of the men became Christians.

Some years ago, I received a call from one of those men. He had located us through the Westover Air Force Base alumni records, where my husband was registered. One of the first things he asked was, "Do you still make those delicious apple pies? In thirty years, I have not been able to find a better one."

To God be the glory! I humbly remember those early days. My first attempt at making homemade biscuits was so bad, our landlord's dogs would not even eat them!

Memories of those initial years of our marriage are still precious. We were nineteen and twenty-one, away from home, and learning to live in a strange and different culture from our southern roots. One thing was certain though. The most important value we shared was our relationship with Jesus Christ. This motivated us to find ways of expressing it in word and deed. After forty-plus years of marriage, this has never changed.

In January 1975, our oldest son, Jonathan, was born. Nothing can describe the joy a mother feels when she looks into the eyes of the child she has carried for nine months. I was overcome with excitement and fear. Would I be a good mother? Could I also balance the responsibilities of motherhood and be obedient to the growing sense of God's call on my life to serve others?

Strengthening My Identity in Christ as a Foundation for Purpose

Shortly after Jonathan was born, Sayres and I visited family in Virginia. It was apparent that my sixty-three-year-old father was in ill health, but I didn't realize he would die only a few months later. My dad was buried on my twenty-first birthday. To make matters worse, within a few short weeks, the Air Force sent Sayres on a one-year remote tour to Korea. I felt lost and totally deserted by God. Fearful and alone, I slowly withdrew, and anger began to fill my soul.

One day, a friend visited me from the little church we attended. As she was leaving, she turned and said, "Kathy, I sense something is not right between you and the Lord."

I was furious. Who was she to judge me? The weeks that followed, however, were a time of deep inner reflection and crying out to God. I faced up to the reality that I was angry with God for my father's death, and my husband's tour in Korea.

Though outwardly, I was strong and opinionated, I was inwardly very insecure. Without a man in my life to give me a sense of worth and security, I felt lost and afraid. I was unaware of it, but I had placed men in the role of God in my life. I repented and asked God to reveal Himself to me and fill the void in my life.

Day and night, I sought the Lord. Like the Apostle Paul, I wanted to "know Him, and the power of His resurrection, and the fellowship of His sufferings" (Phil. 3:10). I hungered for God, and my soul was thirsty for Him. Jesus did not disappoint me. Little by little, He began to reveal His essence and His character. Jesus guided me through the Scriptures. He showed me Galatians 5:22-23, and I experienced God as love, joy, peace, longsuffering, gentleness, goodness, meekness, temperance, and faith, one by one.

A vivid experience illustrates this process clearly. Early one morning while lying in bed, I suddenly heard a man laughing out loud. Terrified, I looked around since no one should have been there except Jonathan and myself. In a moment, I realized the laughing was coming from the Lord Jesus. I was overcome with the presence of God, as He literally turned my sorrow into joy, and I too began laughing.

Later, I read Zephaniah 3:17, "He will take great delight in you, He will quiet you with His love, He will rejoice over you with singing." Like David, in Psalm 51, the Lord had restored the joy of my salvation and was upholding me with His free Spirit.

He allowed me to experience His presence and understand Him more fully. I realized later that all the fruit of the Spirit flow out of love, the essence of who God is.

God next took me to I Corinthians 12 and taught me more. Christ was able to equip the Body of Christ with the "gifts of the Spirit" because the members of the Body are a part of Him. He did not want me to be ignorant of His power and the workings of His presence in His people, because it is God who works in and through us to accomplish His will. It is out of this understanding of God that we can identify the gifts and roles He has given us. The important thing was not whether I was called to a particular position in Christ, but that Christ lived in me. I was to allow Him to flow and move in and through me in whatever way He chose.

These revelations from the Scriptures became the foundation of how I see God. I was now secure in my Father's love. I knew who He was, and who I was in Him. My life was hidden through Christ in God, and I was a new creation, "The old has gone, the new is here" (2 Cor. 5:17).

I was now ready to face the world with confidence and security because I could see through God's eyes, and He had made Himself real to me. As I rested in the assurance of this love, the Lord continued to impress on my heart the truth of the gospel of grace over the next ten months.

CHAPTER 4

Power

Discovering the Power of God and His Grace

Because I grew up in a rural Pentecostal church, I was more familiar with a works oriented salvation. I understood the rules clearly, especially for a woman — no pants, no make-up, no cutting of the hair, no sex outside marriage, no cussing, and a long list of other "do not's."

It was for this reason that I had difficulty coming to know the Lord in the first place. The night I accepted Christ at the Southern Baptist Youth Camp in the summer of 1972, I was concerned I would be unable to please God. I told the Lord I would give it a year to see if He was real. Fortunately, the Lord knew I could not last a day, much less a year, but He had a plan.

Shortly after arriving at Ferrum, an evangelist came to visit us. After a couple of days of teaching, he held a baptismal service in the pool on campus. I wanted to be baptized, knowing this is an act of faith recognizing the death to my old self and the resurrection to new life in Christ.

When I came up out of the water, I was overwhelmed with the presence of the Holy Spirit. I was filled to overflowing and could not contain myself. My praise lifted toward heaven unashamed. Filled with this power, I could now face my fears, knowing Jesus was able to keep me from falling and to present me faultless before His throne (Jude 1:24).

In 1975, as I studied Paul's letters, including the book of Romans, I concluded that what is needed is resting in God and allowing Him to work in and through me. I could not produce the power to do good in and of myself. However, He was able to give me the power to please Him and has given me the power to serve others through the same grace. It was God who was working in me "to will and to act in order to fulfill his good purpose" (Phil. 2:13). My understanding of empowerment became clearer as I looked at the life of Abraham.

> What then shall we say that Abraham, the forefather of us Jews, discovered in this matter? If, in fact, Abraham was justified by works, he had something to boast about – but not before God. What does Scripture say? "Abraham believed God, and it was credited to him as righteousness" (Rom. 4:1-4).

The concept of faith alone was one of the most difficult truths for new Jewish believers hearing Paul's letter, which is apparent in Peter's life. In Acts, God reveals this truth to Peter as He prepared him to go to the house of the Gentile Cornelius. The revelation of God was clear when Peter explained these events by saying:

> Then I remembered what the Lord had said: "John baptized with water, but you will be baptized with the Holy Spirit." So if God gave them the same gift he gave us who believed in the Lord Jesus Christ, who was I to think that I could stand in God's way? (Acts 11:16-17)

Later, however, Paul confronted Peter on his hypocrisy over the same issue:

> When I saw that they were not acting in line with the truth of the gospel, I said to Cephas in front of them all, "You are a Jew, yet you live like a Gentile and not like a Jew. How is it, then, that you force Gentiles to follow Jewish customs?" (Galatians 2:14-16)

Paul wrote, "Now to anyone who works, their wages are not credited to them as a gift, but as an obligation." (Rom. 4:4).

I determined I would live in the gospel of grace because that is where the power resides. I was crucified with Christ, yet, I lived, and the "The life I now live in the body, I live by faith in the Son of God, who loved me and gave himself for me" (Gal. 2:20).

The Holy Spirit came to conform me to Christ's image and equip me for His work. "For it is by grace you have been saved, through faith — and this is not from yourselves, it is the gift of God not by works, so that no one can boast." Ephesians 2:8-9. In vs 10, Paul continues to say, "we are God's handiwork, created in Christ Jesus for good works, which God prepared in advance for us to do." In the Greek, God's handiwork is *poiesis*. In essence, we are the poem God is writing, the instruments in God's hand to do good works.

In Acts Chapter 2, God sends the Holy Spirit when a diversity of people and languages were together. In this new Kingdom, all people would be equal. Paul expounds on this in Galatians 3:28. In Christ, "there is neither Jew or Greek, neither slave or free, neither male nor female." I now had confidence this was all true, despite what the world and the church told me. I knew my Daddy loved me, and I knew He loved all people equally.

In John 4, Jesus displayed this vividly in His encounter with the Samaritan woman at the well. There, Jesus bridged the racial, class, and gender gaps of His society, and as a result, a Samaritan village came to faith, even though His Jewish disciples stood dumbfounded. They were paralyzed by their prejudice while Jesus modeled effective servant leadership.

More and more, my calling was solidified. I could clearly see the evils that fought to destroy God's Kingdom on earth through racism, classism, and sexism, and I was destined to take a stand against them.

Empowered to Bless Others

When the Air Force sent Sayres on the remote tour to Korea for a year, our son, Jonathan, and I were allowed to remain in the military housing units at

Westover Air Force Base in Chicopee, Massachusetts. During the summer of 1976, I decided to visit my family in Virginia. While there, my nephew, who was like a younger brother to me, attempted suicide. I was able to share the good news of Christ with him, and he became a Christian.

Because I was committed to discipleship, I quickly became convinced I needed to apply Isaiah 58 to my life and take my nephew back to Massachusetts with me. He lived with us for the next two years and grew stronger in his faith. When Sayres arrived home in September 1976, he found a transformed wife and an extended family.

In May 1977, the Lord added another blessing to our lives with the arrival of our second son, David. Not long after, the Lord brought a woman to our home who was recovering from an abusive relationship that ended in divorce. She lived with us for a year . . . and eventually married my nephew.

These early years of life and our ministry together laid the foundation of our identity, purpose, and power, and we were beginning to pass them on to others on an individual, one-by-one basis. But what about communities? Could these principles be applied to an entire community? We were about to start learning.

Texas Beginnings

During the summer of 1978, as Sayres was preparing to finish his tour of duty in the Air Force, he and I prayed about what the Lord would have us do next. The more I prayed, the more I sensed an urgency to move to Dallas, Texas. But I kept wondering why the Lord put Dallas on my heart, since neither Sayres nor I knew anyone there. I had never even visited the city, and Sayres had been there only once.

We applied for leave time and headed south, picked up my sister, Alice, and her husband, Sam, in Virginia, and began the long journey to Dallas. We needed to see why God had placed this city on our hearts, and what He might have in store for us.

When we arrived, Sayres began poring over the local newspaper, looking for job opportunities, and I started looking for a mobile home. We only had four days, so we didn't want to waste a moment. I found a mobile home and lot nearby; however, we had two problems. One, he did not have a job, and employment was necessary to get approval for the home loan; and two, Sayres wasn't scheduled to be out of the military for another nine months.

We began to pray, believing that if God wanted us in Dallas, He would open the doors. Sayres describes what happened next:

> I had found an ad for a "Christian" employment agency. I visited the office and found myself being interviewed by a young woman in a huge, open room with forty plus desks, filled with people. The atmosphere was loud and energetic.
>
> As the woman finished my interview, I asked her about her job, and she explained it to me. I said I might enjoy that responsibility and was soon called to another desk by a manager, Bob Murphy.
>
> Bob was a retired Army veteran with an engaging smile who began to ask many questions, "What are your skills? What do you want to do, etc.?" Suddenly he stopped, leaned back in his chair, and said, "Sayres, tell me, why are you really in Dallas?"
>
> Up to this point, I had been going through a standard interview procedure and had said nothing about the leading of God in bringing us to Dallas. When Bob asked me point blank, I decided to just tell the truth. I told him that God told us to come. I didn't know why, but we were here, and I was looking for a job.
>
> Bob smiled, asked me some more introspective questions, and then stopped again, looking at me intently. I will never forget his next words. "Sayres, I have a feeling in my spirit. I believe God did lead you to Dallas. In fact, I believe God led you here, and I'm going to offer you a job, working here, and that is your desk right there."

I was overwhelmed, and still not completely understanding the role of an employment agency. I said "Mr. Murphy, that's great, but what do you do?" After he explained, I asked about the salary, and he said everyone was on commission, including himself. I then shared the two problems: I needed a salary of $800 per month to qualify for the loan, and I may not be available for nine months.

Bob told me to come back in the morning to see some of the other managers and talk about it. The next morning, I interviewed with three others and then found myself with Bob Murphy again. He said the others gave me the nod, so I was hired, and then God showed His miraculous power.

After I left the day before, Bob met with the agency owner who I found out later was not a Christian. Bob shared my story, said he had offered me a job, and then explained our dilemma with the loan. He also proclaimed to this man I had not met, that he thought I would be a superstar in their business, a top producer.

The owner skeptically listened but said he did not pay salaries. Bob Murphy, obviously led by the Lord, told him that if he would pay me a draw of $800 per month and I did not work out, Bob would repay the money out of his commissions! The owner agreed with his manager reluctantly, and, with a letter from Bob stating my employment terms, we were approved for the loan later that day. Kathy and I now knew clearly that God was leading us to Dallas, but we still did not know the purpose.

We returned home, assured that the Lord would make a way for us to get out of the military early so we could purchase the mobile home and move to Dallas where Sayres' new career awaited him. Sayres applied to get out of the military early, but was told his chances were slim due to a shortage in his field. Undaunted, we continued to seek the Lord and, like the persistent widow (Luke 18:3-4), we continued asking, as we made arrangements by faith to move.

At the last moment, when it seemed we had made fools of ourselves, we were alerted that his early dismissal had been approved. Within days, I loaded our two boys and the young woman who would later marry my nephew into our car and headed for Dallas. Sayres would join us within the next few weeks with our belongings. We were about to experience life in Texas.

Sayres started his new job with The Dial Agency just before Christmas 1978, which is a difficult time to begin a new job, especially one that paid on commission. Miraculously, within the first two months, he became top producer. Month after month, he remained at the top, and within six months, we had moved out of our mobile home and bought a house in the Dallas suburbs.

Over the next two years, he continued to be top producer and eventually convinced the owner to let him start a recruiting branch for the firm.

Dudley family portrait in early 1981. Check out the matching outfits!

The girl from "down in the boondocks" was now experiencing the finer things in life.

By 1981, we had moved again, this time into a beautiful four-bedroom, three-bath home in another Dallas suburb. It was then the Lord asked me how I could have three baths when my mother had none. We responded immediately. Along with two of my sisters and their husbands, we built a bathroom in my mom's little two-room home back in southwest Virginia, where previously, she only had an outhouse.

Life was good. We had a beautiful home with a circular drive, and a luxury van sitting out front; we had attained the American dream. At the same time though, we were both passionate about wanting to serve Christ and reach out to the poor. It seemed everywhere I went, there were people in need . . . so I brought them home with me from the donut shop, mall, grocery store, or anywhere I came across them.

Little by little, our house was filled with people trying to get off drugs, prostitutes looking for a new way of life, and those who just needed a hand up. We took them off the streets, discipled them, helped them find jobs, and once they were stabilized, they moved out.

Eventually, we ran out of space, so we decided to set up a ministry and 501(c)3 that would allow us to train other couples, who then could open their homes to those in need as well. Two couples ended up joining us, and Rhema Home Ministries, our first non-profit, was born.

In addition to this in-home ministry, we had weekly Bible studies that were cross-denominational. People came to these studies at our home from all over the Dallas-Fort Worth area. Within a few months, it became obvious we were not very popular among our neighbors, despite our continued efforts to reach out to them. There was probably no one happier than our neighbors when the Lord began to impress upon my heart His desire for us to move to the inner city of Dallas, in order to better serve the poor.

As my children started school, I became increasingly concerned for them. It was clear, with everything we were doing, they were basically living in a "hospital." Though it had been challenging until that point, I had been able to arrange my schedule around our children's needs, as well as those living with us. However, with them in school, it became impossible for me to stay up most of the night counseling others and still be available for our children. I began to seek God for a solution to this dilemma.

In 1981, it was becoming obvious we needed to shut the home ministry down. But the Lord would not let my heart rest. Night after night, dreams of my experiences growing up in poverty ran through my head. I sensed God was asking me to live among the poor, and I struggled. Having spent my whole life trying to escape poverty, this was the last thing I wanted to do.

Like videos, these childhood images of when I felt so much hopelessness and despair played over and over in my mind. I knew the Lord wanted me to respond, but I wasn't sure if I could.

CHAPTER 5

Dallas: Voice of Hope

It was a time of transition and uncertainty. Our Bible study group sought the Lord with us. Many of them had come through our home ministry through the years and were willing to assist us in whatever God had in store.

In 1981, I heard about a ministry in Dallas that was reaching out to the poor. Sayres and I contacted Dr. Ruben Conner, an African American pastor who led the ministry, and shared our burden with him, and he listened. He encouraged us to volunteer in West Dallas with Arrvel Wilson and his wife. We met the Wilsons and began going door-to-door, witnessing with them in the government housing projects.

Dr. Conner later explained that he sent us there to give us a "reality check," with no expectation we would last. We ended up assisting this African American couple for the next year, as they planted a church. During that year, a burden for West Dallas developed as we saw the hopelessness of so many we met there.

Having already practiced holistic ministry through our non-profit, Rhema Home Ministries, I was seeking ways to utilize those principles on a community level. In June 1982, we learned of a conference in Jackson, Mississippi called Jubilee 82, while eating our favorite BBQ at Smokey Johns in Oak Cliff. The conference was sponsored by Voice of Calvary Ministries,

Dr. John Perkins, the father of Christian Community Development in 2019. He and I met in 1982.

founded by John Perkins and led at that time by Lem Tucker. The gathering of national ministry leaders at Jubilee 82 was the seed that eventually became the Christian Community Development Association in 1989. After the four-day conference in 1982, I stayed at Voice of Calvary Ministries for an additional month to study the Perkins Principles of Christian Community Development.

What I learned there impacted me tremendously by giving me a vision of what it could look like when a community was being addressed with a whole Gospel approach, both social action and evangelism. During that month, I also had the privilege of meeting Dolphus Weary. Dolphus was the first indigenous leader to come out of Voice of Calvary Ministries in Mendenhall. We bonded quickly and he agreed to mentor me.

Upon returning home, my call was clear. God was asking us to leave our beautiful suburban home, nice neighborhood, comfortable surroundings, and Sayres' lucrative job. But we struggled with this decision. Little by little, God continued breaking our hearts, and we wanted most of all to be obedient. After much prayer with our Bible study group, we surrendered to God's leading. Within a few months, we were both in full-time ministry and had established Voice of Hope as a non-profit in October 1982.

In November, I read about a woman named Betty in the *Dallas Morning News*. The article shared how she had six children, three boys and three girls, but a devastating house fire had recently killed all three of her girls. I decided to visit her. I introduced myself and asked her how I could help.

Due to the article, she was receiving a significant number of donations. So much stuff arrived that it was literally filling up a vacant lot beside her aunt's home who lived across the street from the fire. Furniture, clothes, everything you can possibly imagine — people's compassion was kicking in, and they were just coming by and dropping items off.

It was Thanksgiving season and people also donated turkeys. She and her neighbor's refrigerators overflowed with turkeys. She even gave some to us. I think the importance of this example is that people were likely giving because they felt pity, but had no relationship with her.

I told Betty, "I'll walk alongside you until people stop giving, and then we can figure out what you need and how to move forward." Obviously, she and her children needed a place to live. She found a house nearby in great need of repair. You could literally see the ground through the floor. It was filthy, and basically uninhabitable, but it was all she could afford. We told her, "If you bring your friends and family, we will bring ours and help you fix this up."

Through this process, we developed a relationship with her sons. We decided to start a children's club on the Amelia Earhart Elementary School playground down the street, going door to door, asking children if they wanted to play. This was met with great suspicion by the parents, but they reluctantly allowed their children to come.

With volunteers from the Bible study, we played soccer and told Bible stories. Soccer was a sport five to twelve year-old boys and girls could enjoy without hurting each other. Never mind I had never played soccer. I bought a book and we learned how. We celebrated every week by giving apples to the kids. For many years, the kids still referred to this time as the soccer and Bible club. Soccer became a bridge to the community.

Betty later moved from West Dallas, and we lost contact. In 1991, I received a letter from Betty, thanking me for loving her and her children through that difficult time.

Relocation To Inner City Dallas

By now, we knew the Lord was asking us to move into the inner city of Dallas, so I began looking for our new place to live. Many thought we had lost our minds, and at times I wondered if they were right. The entire process was very difficult for me. I was more than willing to bring the poor into my house as Isaiah 58 admonished, but I did not want to live in or among poverty again. I had seen and experienced enough poverty in my early years to last a lifetime. However, in the end, we continued to trust God and believe that relocating would be the best way to demonstrate the love of God among those He was asking us to serve.

It wasn't long before I found a house in Oak Cliff. We converted the duplex into a triplex, which meant it could house our family, my nephew and his wife, and two single men from the Bible study who had agreed to volunteer in the new ministry. It took some extensive remodeling to get it ready for occupancy, but the time finally came, and we adjusted to our new abode.

An understanding of our new reality came quickly. In the first month, we heard gunshots in the rear alley behind our house where two men had

That's me, Mama D, with some of the Promise Kids in the early years of Voice of Hope.

wounded each other. Doubts emerged, and I wondered how we could bring our two small boys into such a dangerous community. I simply had to keep my eyes on God's calling for us and believe He would protect us as we continued to move out in faith and obedience. God used what we had: a soccer ball, a Bible, our meager savings, and ourselves.

Voice of Hope Takes Root

In the spring of 1983, after five months of soccer clubs on the streets, we leased and remodeled the smaller of two buildings of an old school that was closed during desegregation. The buildings were being used by Dallas County Community Action (DCCA) which was a part of the War On Poverty programs. A few months before, a group of us had marched around the property, praying that God would give it to Voice of Hope.

That dream became a reality later in 1983 when we purchased the property. We extended the lease of the larger building to DCCA for another twelve months. By the end of 1986, the remodel was complete, and it became the Voice of Hope headquarters and community center in the heart of the neighborhood.

However, our presence and efforts were not appreciated by all the people in West Dallas. Two times, the lug nuts on our van were loosened. It was suspected someone was trying to cause an accident with me driving, without realizing they would potentially cause the deaths of numerous children, including mine, at the same time. The first time, I stopped at a stop sign and the tire suddenly fell off. The second time, I recognized the vibration and pulled over before the tire came loose. We then installed lock nuts on the van. We lived with regular threats, but fortunately, no one acted upon them.

The kids in the community and their families helped renovate the center, creating a sense of ownership. In addition, God brought professionals like Elliott Williamson and his construction company to lead the renovation.

Sayres took this picture, standing on top of the VOH van in 1988. Jonathan is on the back row and David is right in front of me.

We had just finished remodeling in 1986 when Carey Casey, an African American working at Pinkston High School with the Fellowship of Christian Athletes, randomly knocked on the door.

He said to me, "Kathy, where are you from?"

I told him, "Virginia."

He stepped back. "My family is from Virginia. What part of Virginia?"

I replied, "You'd never know where this place is. It's a little hamlet called Barren Springs."

He looked at me in astonishment. "What? *My* family is from Barren Springs."

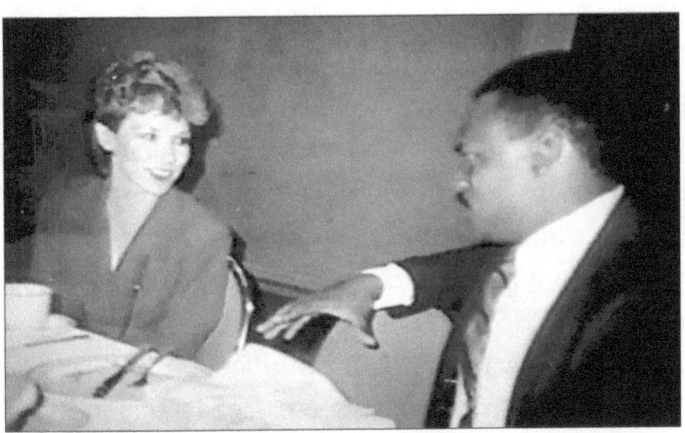

Kathy and Carey Casey at the Voice of Hope banquet in 1986.

Earlier, I related that Barren Springs was a tiny community, racially separated by a creek with a freshwater spring that all shared. As Carey was talking with me, I suddenly realized that when I gave water to the African American families going to church as a little girl, I had been giving it to his family!

I love looking back and seeing the providence of God, and how He does things. Years later, I am grateful to God for allowing me to see how His hand was on my life even before I knew Him. The next time we were in Barren Springs, my husband and I went back across the little swinging bridge, and I introduced myself to his family.

In 1988, I attended a very significant conference that would play a major role in my life moving forward. I was invited to Leadership 88, the vision of Leighton Ford sponsored by the Lausanne Committee for World Evangelization. The primary purpose was to equip young leaders for world evangelism and give them opportunities to build networks with one another.

There, I met two leaders who would have great influence on my life. Dr. Bill Pannell, an African American professor at Fuller Seminary in Pasadena, CA, was introduced to me by Dolphus Weary. He stayed in touch and sent me encouraging notes over the years. Bill visited us in Dallas several times

---

I am an eyewitness to what Kathy has written in her book. Kathy and I began working together when I was serving as vice president of Urban Evangelical Mission. I am an 81-year old African American male born just south of Dallas. My overall ministry experience includes engaging the Global Body of Christ on five of the seven continents and have taught at Dallas Theological Seminary since 1986.

My heart and my head are full of reflections as I look back on Kathy's courage, humility, and effective leadership in those early days. For readers to appreciate the significance of all God used Dr. Dudley to accomplish it is important to understand just how negative and hostile the racially divided blacks and whites in Dallas were in the 1980s. The resentment was high in both directions. And if any existed at all, trust was extremely low. Kathy's most shining achievement to the glory of God, is the manner in which she did this groundbreaking unheard-of thing - Dallas blacks and whites working together. People with wealth entered into close proximity with people living in dire poverty.

– Dr. Willie Peterson, Assistant to the Superintendent, Midsouth Conference, Evangelical Covenant Church

and when I was accepted into the DMin program, I asked him to consider being my doctoral advisor.

Dr. Cathie Kroeger was a professor at Gordon Conwell in Boston, MA and had just co-founded a new organization, Christians For Biblical Equality (CBE). CBE had a display table at the conference. She was the first evangelical theologian I had ever met who espoused biblical equality for women. Some years later, Cathie invited me to join the board of CBE.

During my years at Voice of Hope, we saw God multiply our humble beginning, and it grew into a mature, Christian community development ministry. In addition to a successful youth program, we developed a significant housing program (both new homes and housing repairs), health club, dental clinic, resale store, education programs, and job training programs.

We came to be recognized locally and nationally as a best practice of Christian community development. I was named a "hometown hero" by a local television channel. VOH was featured in 1994 on the national news program entitled, *Eye on America*, and the ministry was featured in *Christianity Today*. We received the 424th Daily Point of Light award under President George H. W. Bush in 1991, and I was selected as one of five of the one thousand Points of Light to speak at the 1992 Republican Convention.

The community was changing and being transformed. Families who had moved out of the neighborhood looking for better housing had returned, which created new possibilities for future leadership. Parents and youth who lived in the community ran many of the VOH programs.

Housing Ministry

Decent affordable housing was a major need in the community. Throughout the 1980s, Voice of Hope was doing minor and some major home repair, but it was clear more needed to be done in housing if we wanted to attract and keep leaders in the neighborhood. To address this need, in 1989, I gathered a group of housing professionals from around the city to look at the issue. Local church pastors, community leaders, bankers, developers, architects, and government leaders came together. I formed a committee to look at how we could address this problem of deplorable housing conditions.

I hired Norman Henry, an African American as our new housing director, and before long, we had secured approval for a sizable government grant to develop new homes in our neighborhood. Increasingly however, I felt uneasy about the strings attached to the grant, which would prevent our openly evangelical stance in the programs. This came to a climax one day in a meeting with bank and government representatives.

I reminded them our main purpose was to "glorify God," as we had articulated clearly from the beginning. We practiced the proclamation and the demonstration of the Gospel in all our efforts.

I prodded the members of our committee for clarification on what was expected of the ministry if we took the funds. I said, "Since we are a Christian ministry, we only hire Christians who agree to a standard of conduct by which we hold one another accountable. For example, if I hire a housing foreman and find out he is having sex outside of marriage, I will fire him. Do you have a problem with that?"

Immediately everyone stammered, and I knew there would be a problem. I said, "If there is a problem with us openly confessing our faith in Christ, we cannot take this money."

It was still obvious to me, however, that the government had a responsibility to the poor, and West Dallas was known for the injustices inflicted upon it. At the time, West Dallas was considered the third poorest inner-city neighborhood in the country. The largest, low-rise, housing project in America was in West Dallas, and a federal lawsuit was pending over segregated housing.

The city had been segregated by race, particularly for where African Americans could live. Ultimately, the West Dallas housing development was declared a glaring example of racial segregation by United States District Judge Jerry Buckmeyer.

The stigma of living in West Dallas was not limited to the dilapidated, federal housing projects. In addition to the lack of stores and banks, a local lead smelter had contaminated the soil, and numerous children and adults were in lawsuit battles due to the consequent health hazards. The plant would have closed long before if it had not been in such a poor neighborhood, where most people felt powerless to respond.

After refusing the grant, I decided to organize a new committee. This time, I selected Christians who represented all the sectors needed to accomplish the work. We gathered at the Voice of Hope Center, and I put a map of West Dallas in the middle of the table.

I began the meeting by saying, "I think it is important for you to know my agenda. It is to dynamite this community with the visible expression of a loving God. In Romans 1:16, the Apostle Paul proclaimed that he was not ashamed of the Gospel of Christ, for it was the power of God unto salvation for all who believed. The word power means, dynamite. I want nothing short of that kind of power to convince West Dallas' people of God's unfailing love.

"We need a show-and-tell gospel, a gospel that is powerful enough and loving enough to meet people's spiritual, physical, and emotional needs. I can think of nothing more tangible than decent, affordable housing. How many of you will join me in that agenda?"

Each of them responded favorably, and we decided to proceed. Over the next two years, each of us worked within our sphere of influence to bring new housing to an area that had been forgotten for a very long time. The banks worked with us on a creative home ownership plan. The city government provided soft, second money through the Enterprise Foundation. A small homebuilder was contracted to build the homes, and VOH provided home ownership classes.

VOH was the vision caster, negotiator, and manager of the partners. Our first home was dedicated in 1991, and by the end of 1994, many new homes dotted the landscape. In 1994 alone, we built over half a million dollars' worth of new homes.

Because we had determined to keep our focus on youth through this time, we hired a housing foreman who worked with teenagers in our program as he built and remodeled the homes in our community. Our goal was not just to build houses, but to develop these young people and give them skills.

The power of the Gospel was seen in a new way, and people responded. Our goal of improving housing through collaboration and helping to build the skills of the youth was being accomplished by creative partnerships with the community, businesses, and government — without compromising the clear proclamation of the Gospel of Jesus Christ.

Point of Light Award

In 1992, I was one of five selected from among the one thousand award recipients of the Daily Points of Light to represent the program at the Republican National Convention in Houston, Texas. I'll never forget that summer. My family and I arrived at my mother's two-room house in

April 1991, President George H.W. Bush presented Voice of Hope the 424th Daily Point of Life award at the Dallas Naval Air Station. I was surrounded by family and friends and we all shared in the honor.

southwest Virginia for a vacation. Mama greeted me by saying, "Kathy, the White House has been calling you."

I thought she was just confused and dismissed it. My sister then entered the house and told me the same thing and handed me a telephone number. I dialed the number in disbelief. After hearing the news, I told the White House representative I would be honored to speak, but I was not a Republican. Upon hearing the gasp at the other end of the phone, I quickly replied, "I'm not a Democrat either. I vote for the candidate I believe will best do the job."

It seemed I was destined to speak at the Houston convention. During the next week, my family traveled to northern Virginia to visit Sayres' mother. Throughout the long, 1400-mile drive back home, I coordinated with the White House on my speech. Though it was assumed they would provide the speech, I insisted upon writing my own. This created an

August 1992, Mrs. Barbara Bush greeted me after I spoke at the Republican National Convention, as a representative of the Daily Point of Life program.

interesting negotiation! We finally agreed that I would write it, and they would have the right of final approval.

Standing in front of 60,000 people, with cameras pointed at me from all over the world, I was reminded of a time, years earlier, when the Lord spoke to me and foretold this event. On May 27, 1979, when Sayres was top producer at his job at the employment agency, as a reward, his company gave him tickets to hear the Jackson Five in Fort Worth. Sayres and I were two white faces totally surrounded in a sea of African Americans.

As I observed my surroundings and listened to the familiar songs, I heard the Lord speak to me. "I will give you more than these." I wasn't clear what the Lord was saying, but afterward, while Sayres and I were eating dinner at a restaurant, I told him what the Lord had said. He looked at me incredulously. From that look, I knew I would have to ponder it in my heart until the Lord confirmed His word. It wasn't my job to make it happen — it was only my job to believe.

For the next thirteen years after that concert, the Lord used me to speak to millions on the radio, and by the time of the Republican National Convention, I had also been on local and national television. As I stood in the Houston Astrodome, I knew God had fulfilled the promise He had given me years earlier at the concert. More importantly, I was fully aware of the grace of God, who could take a poor girl from the country, and manifest Himself in her life in a way that drew the attention of the mighty and the meek. His power was made evident through my human frame.

The success and effectiveness of Voice of Hope in accomplishing its mission was summed up in the comments made by President George H. W. Bush on April 8, 1991, when we received the 424th Daily Point of Light Award.

> I think the name is well chosen, for you bring to the citizens of this corner of Dallas what they need most, and that is a sense of hope, the belief that every community can be reborn and that everyone can succeed.

Having known a life of poverty herself, Kathy Dudley was determined to help others overcome the hardships that she had experienced. And she founded Voice of Hope Ministries in 1982. And when you began, you had only a dilapidated, abandoned school for a meeting place. With hard work and faith in God and in yourselves, you've transformed that building into a thriving community center full of love and support for all who seek it.

Through your programs to enrich the lives of young people and seniors, your literacy and financial management programs to open the door to economic opportunity, and then other related programs, you are reclaiming the community from despair and disintegration. You're making a community whole.

And so, I am very grateful to speak for a grateful nation in saluting you for the strides that you've made. You are real-life American heroes, and all of us are very, very proud of you. And for those out there who say it can't be done, some communities can't be saved, I say to them: You all come to Dallas and see the Voice of Hope Ministries for yourself.

Transition

By the summer of 1994, we were at the peak of our ministry success when Sayres, the boys, and I went to a Pinkston High School graduation ceremony. I watched one by one, as a group of young men and women who had grown up at Voice of Hope walked across the stage.

Then I heard the familiar voice of God speaking to me. "Your time at Voice of Hope is up. You have accomplished the purpose for which I sent you, and there is something else for you to do." As when the ministry journey began, we were at a critical crossroads of both ministry calling and family responsibilities.

I was deeply aware that the demands of VOH had put a strain on our family, and our youngest son, David, had especially suffered. He was

David in 1983, hamming it up with some of his friends from Promise Kids.

detached, depressed, and we suspected he was experimenting with drugs.

When the Lord had called us to relocate into the inner city, our greatest concern had been our boys. Where would they go to school? How would they be received? Would they be safe, and what dangers lurked ahead?

The Lord had quickly calmed my fears by giving me a peace that He had called not only *me*, but also our *family*, including our boys. Now, however, after the intense Rhema Home Ministries years, followed by thirteen years in West Dallas, it was time to reflect.

Had I maintained a balance as a mother and a minister? I was also aware that my wonderful husband had supported me tirelessly for all those years, but I could see that he was weary. What did all this mean? What was God asking of me? How could I leave the ministry in which we had given everything, and maybe too much? It was a time to search for answers. It was a time to seek God.

CHAPTER 6

Texas: Dallas Leadership Foundation

Times of transition are never easy. Leaving VOH after thirteen years of intense ministry proved to be one of the most difficult things I had ever done up to that point. For one, there was the question of how our family would live.

During the VOH years, Sayres had volunteered significant time at the ministry while also working part time in his own business. We had put much of our money into VOH, and he joined me full time in 1992. He could restart his business, but we had little savings.

Our oldest son, Jonathan, was in college, and we were living in a home built for us in West Dallas. It appeared to be the worst possible time to plan to leave, but Sayres and I both knew it was right, and it became official in January 1995.

For a year or more prior, a major paradigm shift was occurring in me. We were primed for growth and VOH was considered a best practice of community development. This was highlighted by a CBS "Eye on America" story. New and restored homes were dotting the landscape, and local leaders had taken ownership of the vision.

However, as I sat on my front porch on Norco Street near the center, watching the neighborhood children play, I was acutely aware of my limitations. Though I had grown up in deep poverty, and often felt discriminated as a female, these children whom I loved would never be able to see themselves in me.

In addition, most of our 600+ volunteers were upper class whites, but few educated, resourced people of color were attracted to VOH as a volunteer. I began to ask why. Did they feel included, invited, or respected? I realized they probably did not. I had not focused enough of my efforts in building that bridge.

I served as a volunteer with Kathy Dudley at Voice of Hope Ministries, a community based Christian non-profit, and as a volunteer and board member of Dallas Leadership Foundation, also a Christian non-profit operating city wide. I was taught to understand, internalize and embrace the key differences between relief work and development work. Relief work is intended to assist individuals with their short term basic needs. Development involves comprehensive and integrated long term strategies and efforts that are holistic in nature, designed to assist and empower individuals to become productive and economically self-sustaining residents and leaders in their own communities.

– Marc Vilfordi, J.D., Imani Bridges Board Member

Realizing the need for a place to connect and learn, we decided to join St. Luke Community UMC, a large, well-respected, African American church in Dallas. During this time, my missional paradigm was gradually expanding from focusing on individuals, to groups, structures and then systems. The BRIDGE framework (explained more fully in following chapters) emerged.

Transitioning Out of Voice of Hope

In the summer of 1994, I joined a group of business, government, and non-profit leaders who were exploring the integration of morals and values into the social fabric of Dallas. During those monthly sessions, I shared my plan to leave Voice of Hope in January. Several influential business leaders in our group challenged me to dream again. They also offered to help jumpstart a new organization with me.

As we met, I sensed their dreams were compatible with mine and agreed. In 1995, with my emerging paradigm, I began working on the establishment of a new non-profit called Dallas Leadership Foundation (DLF).

Through prayer and reflection, I realized that though we had seen great results in West Dallas, the strategy needed to shift to a church-centered model. During this time, I was studying the life of David. His dedication and commitment to bringing the ark of the covenant back to Jerusalem after it was captured by the Philistines twenty years earlier caught my attention.

When David began to reign, he consolidated power as the new king in a united Israel and sought to make Jerusalem the new capital. He realized he lacked one thing — the ark of the covenant, which was in Kiriath Jearim. The first priority of his administration was to provide a proper resting place for the ark, as he realized the ark represented the very presence of God.

Historically and symbolically, the ark of the covenant was a symbol of the covenant between the Hebrew people and their God. David decided to bring the ark back to Jerusalem since the Philistines had captured it.

The ark had been captured by the Philistines as described in I Samuel 4. During the latter part of the period of the Judges, the Israelites decided to carry the ark into battle against the Philistines, hoping it would bring them luck (1 Sam. 4:3). This desecration of the sacred ark enraged the Lord. He allowed the Philistines to win the battle, and they captured the ark (I Sam. 4:5-11).

This action worked against the Philistines, because all sorts of calamities afflicted them, and they decided to return the ark (I Sam. 5:10-12). The

Philistines used a new cart drawn by oxen and sent the cart on its way with a guilt offering of golden rats and tumors representing the plagues that had come upon them since the capture of the ark.

Scripture describes David's techniques in community organizing. "The whole assembly agreed to do this, because it seemed right to all the people" (1 Chron. 13:4). He accomplished this community agreement with his vision by "conferring with each of his officers, the commanders of thousands and commanders of hundreds" (1 Chron. 13:1) before unfolding his plan to "the whole assembly of Israel" (1 Chron. 13:2).

David requisitioned a new cart and oxen to retrieve the ark, and "David and all the Israelites with him went to Baalah of Judah (Kiriath Jearim) to bring up from there the ark of God the Lord" (1 Chron. 13:6).

That evening, they prepared to place the ark on a threshing floor for shelter, but the oxen stumbled, and Uzzah reached out his hand to steady the ark. God struck him dead. David became angry because the Lord's wrath had broken out against Uzzah, "David was afraid of God that day and asked, 'How can I ever bring the ark of God to me?'" (1Chron. 13:12)

He then took the ark to the house of Obed-Edom, the Gittite, where it remained for three months, and "The Lord blessed his household and everything he had" (1Chron. 13:14).

David's second attempt to bring the ark back to Jerusalem is described in I Chronicles 15. His time of reflection with God revealed he had done the right thing, but he did it the wrong way. He said, "No one but the Levites may carry the ark of God, because the Lord chose them to carry the ark of the Lord and to minister before him forever" (1 Chron. 15:2).

This time, he moved the ark in the traditional way, held between two poles on the shoulders of the priests, and he was successful.

The first time, David attempted to move the ark, he copied the Philistines and did not follow the pattern of God. David learned his lesson, and the ark finally rested in its proper place.

As I reflected on this story, I realized I had made the same mistake at VOH, and this was the reason the African American church community had resisted involvement. We had overlooked a valuable lesson and had not appropriately respected the role of African American pastors and the role of the church. I determined to refocus our strategy to a church-centered approach in urban ministry.

Discovering the Identity of Dallas Leadership Foundation

I spent time wondering what God was asking of the Church in Dallas, and what ways we might work together to accomplish a greater good. What were the common dreams that would draw us together to do what none of us could do alone?

To answer some of these questions and give DLF a definitive direction, I decided to do a survey. Often, people get a vision to do things for others and set out to do just that, without asking the most important questions. What is it they want and need? What are they already doing? I determined from the start to listen or do what we call "sitting on the porch" time, using asset-based community development and appreciative inquiry models.

I interviewed Latino gang leaders in East Dallas, mothers on welfare, men and women from various backgrounds, neighborhood watch and block leaders, and even some of the wealthiest people in the city who had tremendous resources and influence.

Through meeting this diverse number of people, I learned they wanted more of what was happening in West Dallas through VOH. These meetings revealed a need and desire for greater minority leadership development, more neighborhood revitalization, and better race relations.

This required a strategy that would link people from diverse parts of the city together in real partnerships to accomplish the vision. This approach would be the only way we could work in multiple neighborhoods at one time and develop the synergy everyone sought. The vision was coalescing.

Youth Initiative

The issue all members of the board agreed on was the need to focus our initial efforts on youth. We had experienced tremendous success at VOH in this area. Of the young people who stayed with us through the years in the Promise Kids program, approximately seventy percent were boys. Our young people did many amazing things. They taught Bible study for younger kids and designed and created their own programs such as an alternate nightclub we titled the Hope House.

Youth remodeled and built homes in the community while learning valuable skills for their future and restored the community at the same time. Most of them graduated from high school in an area that had very high dropout rates. New leadership had emerged in the West Dallas community.

Like VOH, our first initiative at DLF was to focus on youth through an entrepreneurial technology class called E-Tech. Using the church-centered community development model, candidates for the class were sponsored by churches throughout the southern sector. We asked, "Who do you want to sponsor into this program?" The churches and non-profits chose the students, helping to feed their leadership development programs. E-Tech grew quickly and significantly.

Our initial E-Tech classes focused on graphic arts. I hired a talented, highly educated African American to assist me in the design and implementation of the program. His ideas for the program were brilliant. We used E-Tech to bring churches and non-profits together for a common cause.

Though the church or non-profit did not have to pay to sponsor a young person, someone in leadership (a youth pastor or director) was required to attend a monthly luncheon so we could work cooperatively on goals. Those goals were defined together, and the leaders were then responsible to hold the student(s) accountable. This shared leadership model succeeded wonderfully in building networks and friendships necessary in discipleship.

E-Tech was a great opportunity for our family and ministry to merge because it gave me the opportunity to put our son, David, in the program and help him in his journey. He was a natural artist and very interested in graphics arts. Through the program, I could reach out to him and minister to other youth at the same time.

It was even better because one of David's best friends, a Latino, was chosen for E-Tech with his brother. David's friend would probably have been considered the least likely to succeed among the three of them. He took the skills learned in E-Tech and subsequently built an amazing career in technology.

David remained in the program until he graduated from high school and joined the Marine Corps. Even though he continued to struggle for some years, E-Tech was an important bridge for him. I am very grateful to God for watching over my son, and am happy to report that David has grown into a fine man, owns a business, and is married with two beautiful children.

With the help of E.K. Bailey Ministries, we eventually launched a small business offshoot of E-Tech: E-Tech Print and Media. E.K. Bailey Ministries became our first customer. This new business gave the students an opportunity to learn small business operations. In addition, local business leaders visited regularly to help mentor. In time, the business grew and became independent, eventually receiving a significant contract from a large corporation. Later on, it spun off to be a successful for-profit company which is still in operation today.

Greater Acceptance in the African American Community

As mentioned, Sayres and I made a critical decision to join an African American church in 1994. We chose to seek out an influential pastor and sought to build a trusting relationship with both him and the congregation. We decided on St. Luke Community United Methodist Church (SLCUMC), where Rev. Dr. Zan Wesley Holmes, Jr. was the pastor.

Pastor Holmes was one of the most respected leaders in the city, but we joined St. Luke for several reasons. In addition to his leadership, the church empowered women leaders as pastors, they had an obvious concern for the community, and they demonstrated tangible love and concern for children. All these factors strongly resonated with me.

Our time at St. Luke began with just sitting in the pews the first year. As one of the only white couples in the church, our presence was visible. I later learned Pastor Holmes knew who I was and my previous work in West Dallas. That first year, a few members and leaders in the church developed a relationship with us, but I did not spend any one-on-one time with Pastor Holmes. Sitting there week after week, I had to deal with a loss of identity as a leader at VOH in West Dallas, and now beginning again with DLF in the southern sector.

During that year, the Lord was tremendously reshaping my theology on ministry in the city. As stated earlier, the VOH volunteer base was predominately white, middle and upper class with little understanding of our mostly poor, African American and Latino community. Though we lived in the VOH neighborhood, I was increasingly aware of the picture we painted. Being part of St. Luke helped me better understand these discrepancies, but I wasn't initially sure how to correct them.

Even as I was pondering this theological shift, we continued moving forward in adding our first community development initiative. As an organization, we were starting to express the same three circles we currently focus on in Imani Bridges.

When looking for leadership in our community development initiative, I asked the question, "Who are the strongest grassroots leaders already doing work in their communities?" This question led me to Jackie Mixon because numerous people started telling me about her.

She lived in the Ideal neighborhood of South Dallas. She had started a crime watch that eventually developed into a neighborhood association. Persuading her to work with me, however, was quite an effort and process. Over time, and a series of meetings, trust developed between us, and we decided to work together on the revitalization of Ideal and adjacent neighborhoods.

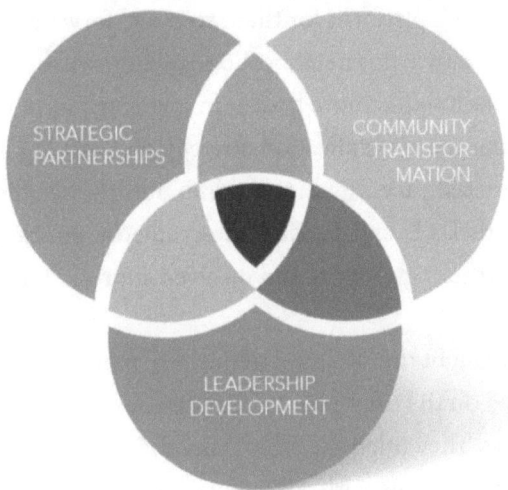

The three-fold ministry emphasis of Imani Bridges, with interconnecting circles representing how each one depends on the other to be complete.

We began garnering support. Business professionals throughout the city were coming together to provide their expertise to remodel an old, dilapidated theatre in Ideal and our plan was to convert it into a community center. Also, a businessman friend of mine from West Dallas found out I was working in South Dallas and donated some lots to us in Bon Ton, an adjacent neighborhood. This jumpstarted the housing plan the community leaders were requesting.

We created a partnership with Habitat for Humanity and within less than a year, we were building new homes in that neighborhood and had begun work on some revitalization initiatives in Ideal. We donated those lots to Habitat for Humanity with the stipulation they must work in collaboration with the local neighborhood association. We pulled in our partners made up of respected Black and white churches, plus numerous businesses. Decisions on who would be recommended to purchase the homes was made by our local partners.

What would have taken years to do on our own was accelerated with this interdependent model. We acted as a catalyst to bring these partners together and create a platform for them to move forward. By introducing Habitat for Humanity to this neighborhood, their work really grew and ultimately, they chose to build more houses in that neighborhood.

It looked like the multiplication strategy was moving ahead successfully and at a very fast pace. Grassroots community leadership were actively participating with DLF, and Jackie had accepted a position on the DLF staff. We were garnering support and received approval for a large foundation grant.

Our efforts caught the attention of the local media and by Easter 1996, we were featured on the front page of the Metropolitan Section of the *Dallas Morning News*. They titled the story "Blood, Sweat and Jesus," and had a huge picture of me praying with volunteers before a major workday. That is when everything changed.

To many African Americans, the story depicted a white woman who had come to South Dallas as the "great white savior," and they were not happy about it. The Black Muslims began to put pressure on the community leaders, and Jackie resigned due to the pressure.

I quickly surmised that the strategy we had begun implementing was not going to work and we were facing a crisis in our South Dallas community development work.

I suggested to Jackie and the leadership in the Ideal Neighborhood that we could assist them in starting their own non-profit, and they could still be a part of the collaborative initiatives we were developing. This show of confidence in their leadership proved to be one of the best decisions we could possibly have made. T.R. Hoover Center was born.

At Voice of Hope, we had created a housing partnership with the Enterprise Foundation, and I realized they were a perfect partner for T.R. Hoover Center to assist them in developing their housing programs. Over the next few years, together they developed fifty new houses in the Ideal Neighborhood. A few years later, T.R. Hoover Center and Jackie and Sheri Mixon were honored by President Clinton as a best practice, and they took the lead on revitalizing their neighborhood in a miraculous way.

Celebration of Hope, where over 800 volunteers helped transform a neighborhood, and demonstrated the power of unity and oneness in Christ.

There really was no road map for what we were doing. What I knew was that for real change to happen in disadvantaged and overlooked communities, grassroots leadership must be respected, and outside resources had to learn to work in true partnership with those closest to the problem. This required patience, humility, and a mindset shift.

Empowered by Black Leadership

An unplanned encounter with Pastor Holmes resulted in an invitation to visit with him. Pastor Holmes said to me, "I know who you are," and then proceeded to ask, "Why did you join St. Luke?"

This was a very fair question. I had come to realize that for African Americans living in a country dominated by white people and white culture, the church was their sacred space of safety. I found out he knew about our success with VOH and that we lived in West Dallas. He knew VOH had received the presidential Point of Light award, that I had spoken at the RNC, and been interviewed on *Eye on America* as a best practice.

I answered Pastor Holmes, "I have lived and ministered in the Black community since 1981 and found a deep connection. I love the worship, how you value community, your empowerment of women leaders as pastors and the way your children are valued in this church. Prioritizing children is huge to me." I paused. "But there's one thing I don't like . . . we've been here over a year, and I have never heard you say anything positive about white people. When you talk about whites, you either say we are evil, the devil, or Pharaoh."

Pastor Holmes was quite surprised at my response because he truly valued equality and did not want us to feel unwelcome. After that day, he was careful to distinguish those of us who benefited from white privilege from those who practiced white supremacy.

Being members of St. Luke, we found ourselves having a front seat to the ongoing issues of racial inequality that our friends experienced in their everyday lives. The reality of this was highlighted on June 7, 1998, when the news exploded with the revelation of the horrific, inhumane incident that took place in Jasper, Texas.

A Black man named James Byrd was murdered by three white supremacists. Byrd was dragged for three miles behind a pickup truck on asphalt. He remained conscious for much of this time and was finally killed when his body hit the edge of a culvert, severing his right arm and head. His murderers drove another one and a half miles before dumping his torso.

Shawn Brewer and Lawrence King were the first white men to be sentenced to death for killing a Black person in the history of modern Texas and became the impetus for a Texas hate crimes law. It later led to passage of the Matthew Shepard and James Byrd Jr. Hate Crimes Prevention Act in 2009 by Congress. As you can imagine, this was a very tortuous event in the Black community.

After Pastor Homes and I met, he decided I was trustworthy. We agreed that St. Luke would partner with Dallas Leadership Foundation on a revitalization project in the Owenwood Neighborhood where the church was located.

The next Sunday, from the pulpit, he asked me to stand up, introduced me by name, and then announced to the congregation, "We are going to partner with Dallas Leadership Foundation, and together we are going to focus on serving this community."

It was like a faucet was suddenly turned on, and I felt affirmed and empowered. When he announced our partnership, other prominent African American churches and community leaders entered this collaborative effort. Leaders from white churches could now interact with their counterparts from Black churches to build real relationships and partnerships. People from northern and southern Dallas, historically separated, suddenly felt comfortable working with us. It was exhilarating and I was so grateful to the Lord to see this happen.

Soon after Pastor Holmes made his announcement at St. Luke, DLF established our second neighborhood revitalization model in Owenwood. We became the platform where the neighborhood association, St. Luke, and others could partner.

Within a short period of time, Owenwood saw drastic changes. DLF and its partners invested several hundred thousand dollars into the project in cash, which was leveraged to over $1,000,000 through in-kind contributions of labor and materials. The money was invested in a crime deterrent project, major and minor home repair for the elderly, neighborhood beautification, and leadership development.

By the second year, home builders saw the transformation of the neighborhood and the involvement of the local church and community. They built a variety of new homes in the area, which brought additional economic stability.

Soon, other African American churches invited us to partner with them on renewal efforts in their communities. Lay leaders from St. Luke mentored counterparts from other churches. Business leaders trained other business leaders who wanted to engage. Lastly, the Owenwood Neighborhood

Association leaders were able to teach what they were learning to others. We were finally finding the multipliers in leadership development and community transformation.

Dallas Leadership Foundation served as a change catalyst for our city by bridging the gap between individuals and groups to address the complex spiritual and social issues prevalent in our communities. By building bridges of trust, we were able to work on dynamic strategies and solutions which produced tangible outcomes and positive change.

We connected transformed leaders by creating structure, events, and opportunities. But to connect these leaders, we first had to find them. We were on the ground, in every sector, in every corner of our community, looking for and developing transformed leaders.

Our broadening network of churches, businesses, and non-profits allowed us to collaborate on city-wide initiatives like Treasures of Hope. This week-long Christmas store was held annually in a donated, downtown space. DLF donors purchased new gifts for the store, where community residents could come one night and shop with dignity, purchasing items at greatly reduced prices. The other nights they would give their time to work at the store, along with white, black, and brown volunteers from across the city. This sense of equality created wonderful relationships, and the laughter and joy throughout the store was contagious.

Another example illustrating this solidarity was the Church Prison Collaborative (CPC). The collaborative was made up of representatives from numerous churches across the Metroplex. We worked together to combine and utilize each other's services, as well as those of several non-profits and government agencies to meet the needs of offenders and ex-offenders when they were released from prison.

Our services ranged from legal and medical services to housing and counseling. Instead of drug dealers, pimps, and gang lords meeting them upon arrival back to their neighborhoods, the church was there with arms open wide. God's people assisted them in their transition back into society. These men learned to give back by serving in various volunteer capacities.

This way, and as a result, they were able to find a true community where they were absolutely accepted.

Programs of DLF such as E-Tech, E-Tech Print and Media, Celebration of Hope, Treasures of Hope, Church Prison Collaborative, Harvest Development Initiative (new home development in the Frazier community), and our involvement in hosting the Christian Community Development Conference are examples of the Body of Christ working together in a way where the sum of the whole is greater than its individual parts. By working together, we leveraged God's resources so more families could be served, and each partner could concentrate on what it did best.

In those early years, we also discovered several minority leaders who had visions, but did not know how to jumpstart them. For this reason, we started a non-profit leaders training program and were able to help eight non-profits emerge. Some are still operating and have grown quite large in Dallas. We learned to help others fulfill their own visions instead of trying to incorporate them into DLF, and this was very fulfilling.

In just a little over seven years, it was nothing short of miraculous as I saw God's people from all over the city come together for the task of rebuilding inner city neighborhoods for the glory of God.

In 2002, I turned the leadership of DLF over to Wil McCall, whom I had hired in 1998, and trained to be my replacement. By this time, we had approximately fifty non-profits and churches in our network; over 200 businesses participated in different projects and the leadership base throughout the city had expanded greatly. Approximately two thousand volunteers participated each year, mostly people of color.

None of this would have happened, however, had I not made a critical decision early on. The original DLF Board, made up of mostly rich, powerful, white males, was not satisfied with how things were going. Increasingly, we seemed to conflict, not with the "what," but the "how" of doing things.

By 1996, I asked all but one of them to resign and serve on an advisory board so I could choose a board more reflective of the grassroots leaders and churches we were working with. I also needed a board that respected my leadership and style.

Looking back, I realized there were several factors contributing to this tension and the resulting decision. First, I don't think these powerful men were used to working with a visionary woman leader who was as entrepreneurial as me. They were used to hiring people to do jobs they wanted done. I was seen more as an employee. I suspect my gender did play a role in this as well.

Had I been male, my strong personality would probably have been seen as more of an asset. On the other hand, being a woman most likely helped me build the relationships across the racial barriers because racial minorities understood I was also familiar with discrimination.

The decision to change the face of our board was a serious one. Though we were allowed to stay in the downtown office space provided through a partnership with one of them, it meant I would lose my salary due to their withdrawal of support. It took another eighteen months before I was paid again, but the decision was well worth it. DLF was owned by its partners and the largest stakeholder was the African American Church. DLF was now free to pursue its dreams because these churches were the majority partners.

This acceptance by African American churches was highlighted during our first fundraising banquet in the spring of 1997, when Pastor Holmes was emcee and Pastor E. K. Bailey the keynote speaker, honoring the work of DLF and affirming my leadership.

DLF was the playground where people could bring their best and not have to carry the whole load. Together, we could do things we couldn't do alone. That was the new model that was emerging.

National Platform

Following Jubilee '82, John Perkins and Lem Tucker periodically gathered a group of inner city ministry leaders at retreats so we could encourage one another and discover best practices. In January 1989, Lem invited thirty-seven people to Chicago O'Hare Airport and asked us the question: "Do we need an association to help us be more intentional in supporting one another and developing young leaders?"

We unanimously agreed to form such an association. Thirteen of us were asked to form the initial board of CCDA and plan the first conference that same year. Tragically, Lem Tucker died of cancer a few months later, before seeing the fruit of the vision. John Perkins became our first board chair and Wayne Gordon was elected President. Now thirty-two years in existence, CCDA is a major influence around the world and I remain a member of the board.

By the mid 1990's, in addition to CCDA, I found myself serving on several other national boards. Jim Wallis, the founder of Sojourners, was forming a new organization, Call To Renewal, and asked me to serve on the board. Call To Renewal was a coalition of Christian leaders united to address the issues of poverty in America.

Dr. Cathie Kroeger invited me to join the board of Christians for Biblical Equality. CBE believes that the Bible, properly interpreted, teaches the fundamental equality of men and women in the home, church, and society. My involvement with CBE expanded my world by connecting me to exemplary biblical scholars from numerous seminaries around the country.

In 1997, I was chosen to speak before a U.S. Congressional hearing and participated in a simultaneous symposium on the empowerment of the poor in America. This was a great honor.

I also became involved in other organizations and networks like the Council of Leadership Foundations, International Urban Associates, and Mission America. Some may say, why were you involved with so many organizations? Quite honestly, it was because each of them provided a part of what I believed God was teaching me, and eventually, the collective knowledge gained would influence the BRIDGE framework.

CHAPTER 7

Just Cause

I am a firm believer in leadership development. It is the responsibility of every generation to prepare others to follow their calling. With both VOH and DLF, I was intentional to seek out and identify leaders to invest in. From the beginning, I planned to transition each organization to leaders of color who would carry the vision.

Turning over an organization once established can be incredibly challenging, and for me, it was no different. I felt the loss of my identity and ability to earn a salary. Having done that at VOH, God was now asking me to do it again.

In 2002, when Wil McCall became executive director of DLF, I continued to serve for eighteen months as board chair. After Dr. Ray Bakke found out I was planning to transition out of DLF, he strongly encouraged me to apply to become a Doctor of Ministry student under him at Northwest Graduate School which later became Bakke Graduate University. He was handpicking students from around the world to study transformational leadership for the global city.

I told him, "That's wonderful! It's a dream I've always had, but I can't do it." I had never finished college, let alone a masters, and was certainly not qualified for a doctoral program.

Dr. Ray Bakke leading our DMin cohort in Guangzhou, China in 2003.

With his recommendation, the school invited me to apply. The uniqueness of this three-year, intensive program was its emphasis on mid-career ministry professionals who would learn together, with classes meeting in cities around the world. I had to create and submit a very comprehensive portfolio of my ministry history, awards, training materials, etc. to the Academic Affairs Committee. After review, they accepted me into the program in the summer of 2002 on probation with other stringent requirements.

Though I was understandably fearful of entering a prestigious academic environment, I determined from the start that my work would be exemplary. I asked my friend Dr. Bill Pannell, an African American professor and Assistant to the President at Fuller Seminary, to be my doctoral mentor. He replied that he had just recently prayed, asking God if he could mentor young Black men. Instead, God sent him a white woman.

Dr. Bill Pannell, my doctoral mentor, in one of our many sessions during my studies.

Bill agreed to work with me, and I felt the need to move to Pasadena, CA where he lived. Sayres and I took another leap of faith and relocated in December 2002. By doing this, I made myself accessible to him to provide oversight for my studies, since I did not have the necessary academic background, but wanted my work to measure up to Fuller standards. Bill helped me with this tirelessly for three years. I will forever be grateful to this wonderful man for walking alongside me during this journey.

In June 2002, I arrived in Seattle, with thirty-six students from across the world for the first two weeks of courses. One of the first challenges for me as a new doctoral student was to begin contemplating what my dissertation would focus on.

During the second week, we traveled to 16th Street Baptist for class. The senior pastor, Dr. Les Braxton, was our teacher for the day. His presentation was powerful and challenging. I felt quite comfortable, as it reminded me of my home church in Dallas.

Dr. Braxton gave a handout to guide us through his presentation on Black church history. His teaching style was thought provoking, but it was the issue of reparations that got my attention and stirred me the most. He asked, "Will the white church miss this one like they did on slavery and civil rights . . . or will they get behind it?"

I suddenly knew what I wanted for the subject of my dissertation. The paper would address the continued inability of most white and Black Americans to build genuine, healthy relationships and the ongoing effects of a racialized society. Through their tremendous suffering, I believed God had uniquely prepared African Americans "for such a time as this" to assist the rest of us in moving toward a more just world in the future.

Discerning Christian leaders were needed to provide a unified voice of hope in our divided world. The building of this "fellowship" in the context of addressing the issues of reparations for African Americans was what I felt called to do.

The way America has refused to deal with the legacy of slavery is unfinished business and is at the very heart of our inability to get to the "beloved community" Dr. Martin L. King, Jr. talked about. I wanted to accomplish something and had an idea. What if we could get African American church leaders across the nation to join in an economic empowerment initiative that could be a prophetic and practical response to America's unwillingness to "do what was just and right" for a people who had been so wronged?

This would require an organized and unified response from the African American church community. The idea could potentially produce significant dollars in a short amount of time. We would call the project "Just Cause," based on the Scripture in Amos 5:24, "Let justice roll down like a river and righteousness like a mighty stream."

I began to strategically share my dream with friends and contacts made over the years, serving on numerous national non-profit boards. The response was incredible and extremely supportive. One leader responded, "This could be the next freedom train."

Another said, "This should have happened yesterday," and he pledged his support. I was hopeful, because these key leaders had the ability to influence and potentially mobilize millions of people for a cause that could change lives.

More importantly, it gave all of us, particularly the African Americans, a way to respond. Rather than being angry, feeling hopeless and despondent, we could do something about our convictions. We formed the "fellowship" to brainstorm on potential ideas that included education, economic empowerment, and events.

Eventually, I dreamed of offering white people and others the same opportunity to join us and move towards building a new future where all God's people could work together for justice, righteousness, and peace. This vision and cause seemed to strike a chord with these leaders.

There was an obvious problem though: I was white. Realizing this, my immediate response was to hand the vision off to different African Americans whom I thought could implement the dream, pledging my continued involvement and support. Eventually, it became apparent this was not going to materialize.

Several of them suggested that the only way this vision could come to fruition was for me to carry it toward implementation, and I agreed to try. For months, I attempted to arrange a summit so the core members of the group could make decisions on how we were going to proceed. The next spring, six of us finally met at Fuller Seminary.

After that meeting, we decided to move forward and start a non-profit that could house the bigger dreams of the team, as well as Just Cause. Everything seemed to be going well until it became clear to me that I was expected to do the job until, as one attendee stated, "a qualified and willing African American could take over."

Though willing to help someone else implement the vision, I didn't like this plan. I felt a total lack of empowerment. It reminded me of an incident years ago while I was still president of Voice of Hope. A representative of one of our major donors said to me, "Kathy, the reason God is allowing you to do what you are doing in West Dallas is because no man would go."

I responded by saying, "If I am doing what some man wouldn't do, then that is not fulfilling to me. I want to do what God called me to do. Furthermore, I believe that is exactly what I am doing."

Twice before, I proved my willingness to turn organizations over to indigenous leaders, but this felt different. There seemed little concern for how difficult such a decision was to me. I felt used instead of loved. I wanted to accomplish what God had uniquely prepared me for, not what someone else was supposed to be doing. Having attempted numerous times to give the vision away, I was prepared to support someone else, or be fully empowered to take the lead, but I was not willing to embark on this journey with the expectation that I would be a temporary place card.

I felt that my being a woman made this suggested arrangement seem appropriate to the others. Beyond the gender issue though, my visibility as a white person, leading this type of prophetic movement, would probably be embarrassing for African Americans. I had to step back and ask, "If God gave me the vision, why could I not implement it?" With this confusion, I decided to slow everything down until I heard from God.

CHAPTER 8

Nigeria and the Birth of Imani Bridges

This turn of events created a dilemma for me with the dissertation. In the face of the reality that the gathering of this fellowship and the Just Cause project were delayed and perhaps non-existent, I decided to refocus. From the beginning, it was apparent this project was much bigger than my Doctor of Ministry.

There was a tension between my being a visionary activist, accustomed to starting things, and learning how to satisfy the research requirements for the DMin. It was the proverbial struggle between process and product. Considering this new reality, a decision would have to be made on a new direction for my dissertation, which was soon to be revealed.

In November 2003, Ray Bakke received an invitation to teach a masters course at West Africa Theological Seminary (WATS) in Lagos, Nigeria the following January. He was unable to attend and asked Dr. Gwen Dewey to go in his stead, and he asked me to co-teach the class for course credit. My first trip to Africa was a fulfillment of a long-desired dream. I asked Sayres to come with me and within six weeks, we were in Nigeria.

The students in the class were composed of seventeen African bishops/church leaders from three countries and numerous denominations and theological perspectives. Many of them had not met prior to enrolling. This was the final course in a special, three-year program created for them, entitled Church & Society. For my presentation, I decided to use this opportunity to test the theology and framework of the BRIDGE, which I will explain fully in later chapters.

The first day, I wasn't slated to teach; just participate and listen. But as we were getting to know each other, and Dr. Dewey was teaching, a discussion arose about African Americans. In unison, the bishops expressed negative comments about them. I sat in shock, contemplating my thoughts, but I knew I had to speak. We would later realize this would be a defining *kairos* moment.

I raised my hand reluctantly, and Dr. Dewey acknowledged me. I said, "Gentlemen, I know you are great leaders. I've heard your stories... but I've lived, worked and worshipped in the African American community for almost twenty-five years, and I haven't heard one of you say anything I think is true."

The Bishops Class in January 2004. The Imani Bridges journey began here.

Teaching the bishops during the 2004 class.

I thought, *Did that actually come out of my mouth? How will they respond when I teach tomorrow?* The bishops seemed perplexed, but now I had their attention. An ensuing discussion went on for some time.

After class, Bishop Wilson Badejo, the head of the Four Square Church for West Africa, overseeing about 2500 churches, engaged me personally to continue the conversation.

Sometime later, Sayres approached us. Bishop Badejo threw his hands up in the air and looked at him. "We love your wife!" he exclaimed. Now I knew I could teach the next day and they were ready to learn.

Right away, God used my weakness to break down walls. I quickly learned that though the students were at the end of their program, they still used their formal titles and last names in addressing one another. I could not pronounce their last names though, so I asked if they would mind me using their first names, to which they agreed.

A small group discussion after one of the teaching modules. I was awed at the intellectual and spiritual level of discourse among these men during class.

We wrote their names on paper placed in front of each of them. That quickly changed the entire tone of the room. In my weakness, there came strength, as titles and formalities fell away. The bishops would tell me later that this simple act opened them up to experience a new ability to relate with each other that has continued to this day.

What I also didn't know was that each evening, the bishops were discussing what I had taught each day and trying to decide if it was biblical and could be applied in their context. One teaching was from John 17, where Jesus prayed for His disciples to be one, and through their unity, the world would know that God sent Jesus. I have always called this "answering the prayer of Jesus."

By the end of that week together, the bishops asked me if I would help them to see how they could impact society through their churches, not just individually, but collectively. This was the seed beginning of the new Imani Bridges. God worked in amazing ways during that week. He broke through the cultural and theological barriers and set in place relationships that would change the course of my ministry.

In the class at WATS in 2004, the most important thing that came out, as if it was a voice from above, was that you can achieve much more by working together. Dr. Kathy Dudley made it so easily achievable by the way we got to interact amid ourselves. These many bishops and senior pastors, church leaders, working on a first name basis, interacting, looking at what each other is doing, as if that is what they also are doing, which is the case; void of competition.

–Pastor Peter Egho
Nigeria Director, Imani Bridges,
Retired Provincial Pastor Redeemed Christian Church of God

In May 2004, I decided to visit Dr. J. Alford Smith, Sr. in Oakland, California, one of the leaders who had agreed to journey with me for Just Cause. My purpose was to update him on the meeting at Fuller since he was unable to come, and to share with him the experiences of my recent trip to Africa.

After he viewed a video I had produced from the trip, he looked at me intently and said, "Kathy, it is obvious what the Lord has done. You have been running around the country trying to bring us African Americans together and God has given you a Macedonian call to Africa."

I was beginning to think he was right because I had already received two invitations to return to Nigeria to teach the things I had shared in class at pastors' conferences. Other students sent encouraging e-mails such as this one.

My beloved Sister,

I bring you hearty greeting from Nigeria. I am so glad God took you back to your base in the U.S. after your most useful missionary trip to Nigeria. Kathy, permit me to say that you really impacted my life and ministry. Not only by the substance of what you taught us but also the passion with which you put your thoughts across. I can't stop thinking about you and about what I heard from you and watched in the video clips. You did not just teach us; you imparted your spirit on us. My whole desire and prayer now are how to put into practical use what you challenged us to do. The simple truth is I keep hearing the echo of your voice.

What I have done so far is to redefine our focus as a church. We have now determined to engage our community with the view of seeing to its eventual transformation. While I pray to get a clearer leading on how to do it, we have started doing something on a small scale. This Saturday, the 14th of February, five hundred branches of my ministry in Nigeria will embark on a program of feeding the hungry and clothing the naked in our immediate environment. This is a way to sensitize them on the need to prayerfully and deliberately confront the real problem of our society which is mass poverty.

I would need you to pray for me. I am now your disciple. As soon as I come up with anything tangible, I will get you informed so you can advise me. Thanks for coming to Nigeria. I am praying that God will give me the opportunity to visit the U.S. Whenever I am able to come, I will surely get in touch with you.

Another participant wrote:

Dear Kathy,

Thanks a lot for your encouraging mails. God has brought you in our lives through our class in WATS and I see beyond that as I see

God using you to mend lives, lift the downcast, bind the brokenhearted and give hope to the hopeless in this part of the world. I believe that the Lord will make all grace abound toward you. Remain blessed and blessed in the Lord.

I immediately began the formation of Imani Bridges to provide an organizational structure for the work God was calling me to in Africa.

Imani Bridges was birthed in seed form at the end of the bishops' class, but it would take many years, and several phases, for it to become what it is today.

CHAPTER 9

Phases One and Two of Imani Bridges

Imani Bridges, as we know it today, was not planned out in a typical fashion, but emerged over many years of trusting relationship building. So far, we've gone through three phases in our journey.

Phase One

During the first phase, I was still a student and some of the bishops invited me back to Nigeria to teach at their pastors' conferences. This lasted about eighteen months, during which many of them met with me and we continued this learning journey together. For one conference, I saw my picture on billboards next to them. They were expecting me to speak to large crowds. I realized that was not going to be the way to influence and change society. I needed to focus on these leaders. If they did not buy into an understanding of the unity of the body and the BRIDGE framework, other efforts would be useless.

As the bishops and their pastors continued to learn from me and from each other, we saw them start to impact society through their churches in

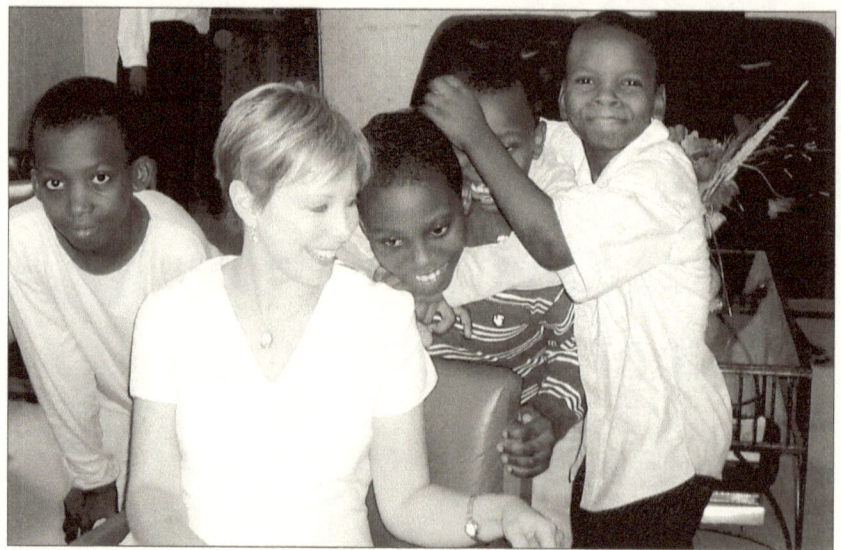

I love the freedom and joy of these Nigerian boys in 2004.

wonderful ways. One example is from Rev. Peter Egho, a member of the class. He was a key leader in the largest denomination in Africa, and one of the largest in the world — an indigenous, African denomination called Redeemed Christian Church of God (RCCG).

Peter invited me to teach to a group and then attend their annual conference in December 2004. This gathering had over five million people in attendance, a sea of humanity I cannot describe. I was on the stage watching amazing miracles happen right before my eyes.

A few years later, the general overseer of the denomination approached Peter and said, "We have to figure out how to have clean water. Let God show you what to do."

This was a chance for Peter to use what he had learned in class and be a model of the church changing society. One amazing part of this story is that Peter was trained as an oil-field mechanical engineer and had never done any work with water purification. However, Peter prayed for wisdom, and

The municipal water system designed and built by Pastor Peter Egho at the RCCG Redemption City. His brilliant work provides clean water to millions.

God gave him an ingenious solution of how to make use of the resources already on the property.

He created a municipal water system that provides clean water for millions, and this allowed for the creation and development of an entire city with modernized, underground plumbing and clean water. The new city and water system are operated by the church.

Other leaders from the class were also doing projects which were impacting society around them. I continued to travel to Nigeria to teach and meet with them.

I was also trying to figure out how to continue with Just Cause in the U.S. We were organizing in Pasadena, California, and getting many people involved and willing to work with me toward a vision for unity. We had a small planning group and were trying to integrate my ideas with Just Cause with what would become Imani Bridges.

I was using an analogy of an airplane to help the Nigerians and Americans understand the Imani Bridges vision. It had to be a space big enough for the body, something that could move us from place to place, and it had two engines (education and economic empowerment).

In 2005, I had a dream. I saw a group of people flying to Africa. We had barely gotten airborne when the plane crashed. I realized this was God showing me we weren't ready to take off yet, and this vision would require more time. Everything I knew, and everything I had done before was not yet enough to take us where God was leading.

Soon after, the idea of combining Just Cause and Imani Bridges fell apart. Members of our planning group began to drop out, and I knew we had to pause everything. It all seems clear now, but when God is creating and developing something new, like Pastor Chuck Swindoll says, sometimes it's "three steps forward and two steps back."

The airplane dream was pivotal in the emergence of Imani Bridges. It helped me realize that the tools I had used in the past were going to be insufficient for this new journey. It had taken fourteen years for VOH to come into maturity and be celebrated (*Eye on America,* Point of Light Award, speaking at the Republican National Convention, etc.).

I had spent seven years with Dallas Leadership Foundation, and the ministry had experienced great success and recognition. With Imani Bridges though, God allowed my original idea to crash, because it was going to be a slow journey of building trust; not just between myself and the Nigerians, but also among the Nigerians themselves.

I needed to wait on the Lord to give direction and then God opened another door.

Phase Two

After I graduated from BGU in 2005, Ray asked if I would become professor of African Studies and Africa Area Director for the school. I laughed and said no, and he asked why.

I replied, "I have been in the African American community for many years and I would not dare become a professor of African American studies, let alone African studies."

After sharing Ray's invitation with the bishops though, they insisted I should accept. I relented, on one condition. Some of them would become my doctoral students and we would figure out an appropriate curriculum together.

Graduation day at BGU, June 2005.

2005–2009 was an interesting and important period where several of the bishops, plus other Nigerian leaders became students in the doctoral program. In 2006, I took my first class of African students to visit Badagry. Most of them had never been there.

In 2004, I had requested the missionaries from WATS take Sayres and I there, as it had been a West African slave port. Our journey was delayed in sweltering heat two hours by police along the road, saying we needed our original passports and not a copy — they were looking for a bribe.

When we finally arrived at the small, slave relic museum in Badagry, it was late, and we paid someone to open it and show us. It was very impactful, but in the city itself, I will never forget the feelings of darkness and hopelessness that enveloped us.

Now I was back with students in 2006. I had them research the slave trade and listen to the history. I learned that in some cases, Badagry was such an unfavorable post for church leaders that bishops sent there by their denomination were being punished. I wanted my students to see beyond Badagry's infamous history and have hope for this city.

What's kept me involved is the reality that I could see value in the relationship as an African American, and those who are in Africa. The fact is we know nothing on any kind of scale about one another, and most of what we know is incomplete. One of the interesting things about African Americans is, from a history standpoint, we don't even know our own history. On a broader scale, most of us, at some point and time in our lives, want to know where we're from.

— Maurice King, Business Owner, Board Chair Imani Bridges

During these early years, the bishops and I realized we needed an official organization, Imani Bridges, for any initiatives not related to the BGU program. IB was formed as a non-profit organization in 2005.

Our first major collaborative idea was to launch a seminary in 2007, with the bishops themselves creating the program, budget, and strategy. We raised funds and hired a Nigerian who had just graduated top of the PhD class from a very prestigious seminary to be Chancellor. That person proceeded to embezzle the funds and start a separate program.

This became a trying season. I was even questioning if God had really spoken to me about what we were pursuing. Would our diverse fellowship stay together when times became difficult? Thankfully, despite our disappointments, we kept on our journey. What never changed during those difficult days was the fact that we had fellowship times and retreats, sharing of ideas and mutual learning. These leaders then took new ideas into their denominations and produced great results.

From 2009–2013, the world economy was in deep recession, but our fellowship remained strong. I traveled to Nigeria and many of them visited us in our home in Texas after we had returned from California in December 2008. Though it was a slow season, it was very valuable.

Years later, that same Nigerian man that embezzled the funds from IB would reach out to me, expecting that the Imani Fellowship had long ceased. He requested I become the president of his new organization. I explained that I was not interested in serving in that role.

He apologized for his wrongdoing and admitted that much of the content of his training programs was a result of Imani Bridges. He then asked if he could join our group in Nigeria in hopes of being able to use our broad denominational membership to market his school and training programs.

I explained that the decision was not mine alone and that he needed to meet with the Fellowship and apologize and ask if they were willing to embrace him. After a lengthy process, we all concluded that he could not be trusted and denied his request.

Some of the Best Practices of Phase Two
Bishop Sam

Soon after the first trip to Nigeria in 2004, Sayres and I attended a Purpose Driven Church conference for global leaders. The room was filled with diverse leaders from around the world. We decided to look around for a table with Nigerians and sat down with a young leader, Sam Airiohuodion, who not long after became General Overseer of his denomination.

We told him about our recent trip and showed him a picture of the bishops. He was stunned, for there in the picture was his elder relative, Peter Egho. Peter had formerly been a Nigerian government official, and has followed a call into ministry, where he was now leading two hundred and seventy churches.

With Nigeria's very hierarchical and social class-driven society, there was no way Sam would have been able to fellowship directly with Peter, even though they were family. Because of my theological belief in equality, and since I had taught that principle to the bishops, we invited Sam to join our fellowship meetings. Sam has proven to be an invaluable and dedicated member of the Imani Fellowship since then.

Sam was affectionately given the title of Baby Bishop because of his age, and he became one of the best implementers of the BRIDGE framework principles in his denomination. When the group decided to begin an economic development initiative, the decision was made by the Fellowship to invest in Sam.

Bishop Sam Airiohuodion

Three grants were made: a micro-lending grant to launch a motorcycle taxi business, a grant for his church's primary school, and a gift to help subsidize some of his rural pastors so they could establish new churches in remote areas. Sam has proven time and again his trustworthiness and willingness to be accountable to the group.

For several years when I traveled in Nigeria, he would stop everything and travel with me. This was extremely beneficial for me as a white foreigner in Nigeria. I am so grateful to Sam for his sacrificial care.

In August 2004, after speaking at a pastors' conference in Owerri, Sam took me to his remote village of Ekpoma, about six hours' drive from Lagos over dangerous roads. There I met his aging father, now blind, who had founded the denomination which Sam is now overseeing. After we talked, it seemed his father saw in my words and vision something ahead, that neither Sam, nor I did at the time.

He told Sam, "Do whatever she tells you to do." Sam remains an amazing blessing to Imani Bridges.

Water

Clean water is one of the greatest needs in the developing world. I shared earlier about Peter Egho building the municipal water system. Every time I visit and see that magnificent system, I thank God for giving him the wisdom to accomplish that.

Another member of the fellowship commissioned a group of businesspeople in his denomination to come up with a clean water solution. They developed a filtration system, and soon they were packaging water in small, plastic sachets for locals. Hotel owners in the city found out about the enterprise and asked them to develop a bottling plant to supply water to their hotels, and they did. That business is still in operation.

Another member of our Imani Fellowship created equipment using solar technology that can be taken into rural areas and used to provide clean water for people who have none.

Other Initiatives

These extraordinary leaders just kept creating new ideas. One church started a credit union with a micro-lending program, specifically for women entrepreneurs. Another did an innovative, solar energy program. Another founded an orphanage. These Nigerians had ideas, were sharing their best practices with others, and were learning how to multiply and provide impact within their environment.

Even though they had amazing accomplishments, individually and in denominations, they were still not working in unity, collectively, fulfilling the prayer of Jesus we had discussed many years before.

A New Day

In 2013, nine years after our original class, we were having an Imani Fellowship meeting in Lagos. The Lord began to make it very clear to everyone present that we had not done what He had asked us to do in 2004 — unite across our denominations and differences, love one another, and walk in unity, and work collectively to reveal the Kingdom of God. Fulfill the prayer of Jesus!

Jesus was the incarnation of God, revealing who God is. With His example, we determined to incarnate the vision of Imani Bridges, and model how the church should look in unity and love.

At this meeting, we decided a more targeted focus was needed and a place to incarnate the vision, much like when Jesus came to show us what God is like. This vision had to be incarnated in a place where people would look and say, "That's the church, the church united."

In 2004, I had said to them, "If you really want to reach the world with the Gospel, then let's answer the prayer of God." That was the original vision and goal that had held us together. Now we needed to implement it.

In 2014, we formally defined our vision statement, based on John 17:23. From that verse, we developed the following statement.

Vision Statement

We envision God's people connecting globally and leveraging our collective spiritual gifts and resources to be agents of transformation in our world.

We believe these words and pray that churches everywhere will implement them. Who sits in the chairs or pews of the churches when the doors are open? Business leaders, non-profit leaders, grassroots leaders, and government leaders. Every sector of society is sitting in our churches. All the resources to transform society are in the churches if we can only mobilize them.

I remember when I shared this with Sam back in 2004. He loved it and thought it was wonderful. However, he also thought it would be impossible in Nigeria, with all the tribal and church divisions. There are 260 tribes and languages in Nigeria and over 500 dialects — a place of huge diversity in a nation of over 200 million people. Now Sam is one of our greatest examples of its application.

Vision Exemplified in Vanuatu

In 2015, a year after initiating this vision in Badagry, God decided to show us the power of this network halfway around the world. In 2012, Peter Egho was asked by RCCG to plant churches in Vanuatu. Vanuatu is a chain of eighty islands approximately 1,000 miles off the northern shores of Australia. It was a forty to forty-two hour trip one way, each time Peter traveled there from Nigeria. By 2015, he had planted twelve churches in Vanuatu, and established key relationships with government leaders.

In 2015, Cyclone Pam struck Vanuatu with ferocity. It literally destroyed these little islands — churches, homes, clinics, schools — everything. RCCG rebuilt their churches and the Vanuatu president's home. Then I received a call from Peter.

He asked, "Don't we have a medical supply partner?"

"Yes, they are in McKinney, Texas," I replied. (Our team had hand carried medical supplies on our first mission week in 2014).

"Do you think they would give us medical supplies to restart the hospitals in Vanuatu?"

Peter's understanding of ministry had been transformed, and he could now see that bringing transformation to society was just as biblical and just as spiritual as building churches.

But to make this medical supply donation a reality, God had to activate His body, literally all over the world. Our medical supply partner, Mission Regan, donated almost $500,000 worth of medical supplies, but how did we get them to Vanuatu?

Getting the medical supplies to Vanuatu was clearly a global effort, highlighting the Imani Bridges network.

A local logistics expert had connections that reserved us a shipping container. We have a Nigerian American friend who pastors a church on the south side of Chicago. A member in his congregation knew someone in Nigeria who was a friend to the president of Vanuatu. Through this personal connection, all our port fees were waived upon arrival.

It took us a year to completely work out the logistics, but for only $5,700, we shipped a container of medical supplies of almost half a million dollars to this very remote location in the ocean. The people of Vanuatu saw that it was God's people who had done this. After the medical supplies had been distributed to the hospitals, the president of the country, an Anglican, told his citizens, "This is the kind of church you should go to."

This remarkable event was a clear example of how the Lord used His people from across the globe, working in unity, to bless suffering people and reveal the love of Jesus Christ in a very tangible way. Imani Bridges is not a relief agency, but regardless, God used us there in a miraculous way. We give Him glory!

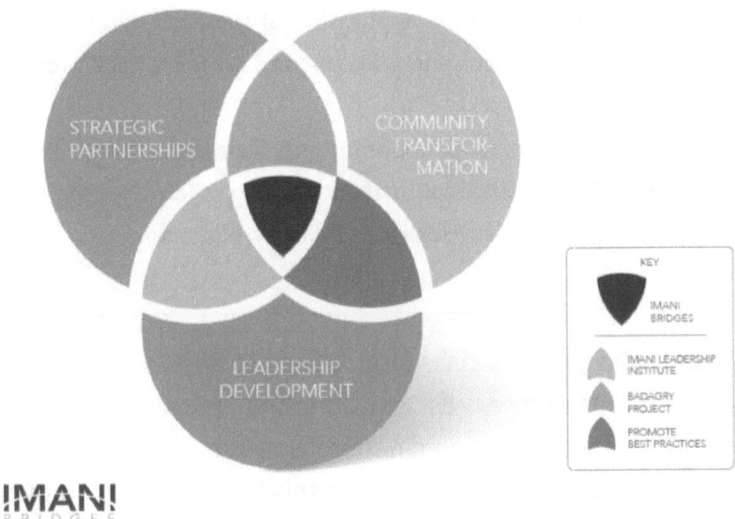

The Imani Bridges Mission

Mission

In Imani Bridges, we are both vision and mission driven. As you can see from the graphic, we focus on three things: Leadership Development, Strategic Partnerships, and Community Transformation. We have clearly identified our primary customer as denominational church leaders — leaders who are already recognized and supported by masses of people in their churches and communities.

Strategic Partnerships is the Imani Fellowship of leaders. We meet regularly to share, fellowship, strategize, exchange ideas, and learn from each other. One of the leaders in the Imani Fellowship may bring in someone else to be a part of the Fellowship (a businessperson, etc.), but our priority is to provide space for equipping the pastors who will then equip the saints.

Leadership Development has been a few different things, but at this point, besides modeling and mentoring, it mostly consists of what we call the Imani Leadership Institute (ILI). We have a team of Nigerians and Americans who teach on two different tracks. First is the Church and

Society track that focuses on the application of the BRIDGE framework through the church to impact society. Second is a Business track, where we teach various business skills.

The last circle in the mission is Community Transformation, where we put it all together. It is the incarnational outworking of Jesus' prayer in John 17. Our first "playground" as we call it, is Badagry, Nigeria.

Our singular aim from the class in 2004 was to answer the prayer of Jesus, that we may be one, as Jesus and the Father are one. Imani Bridges brings together denominations and organizations to work together as the Body of Christ. We do this without thinking of the differences we have in practice and beliefs, because Christ unites us. Leaders see themselves as servants of the people. Working together, we are a platform of equality, with large and small churches gaining equal respect. That is how Imani Bridges has influenced Nigeria. I long to see this fully materialize and I have decided to serve Imani Bridges in any way I can be helpful to bring this aim to fruition.

– Venerable Dr. George Adeyeye, Anglican Communion, Lagos

CHAPTER 10

Phase Three: Badagry and ILI

Looking at our three circles, we started with building strong Strategic Partnerships, and began the planning for Leadership Development training. The focus on Community Transformation brought it all together and became exemplified through our work in Badagry.

With every organization that I started before Imani Bridges, it began from the grassroots and moved up. With Imani Bridges, our biggest challenge was whether we could start at the top and move down. I wasn't sure. One thing was clear. For our work to take root in Badagry, and for transformation to happen, the local churches, spanning the same spread of denominations as the bishops' class, had to catch the vision for unity and equipping the saints. I can honestly say that has taken place.

We chose Badagry for two reasons. One, it's a Nigerian city of firsts. The first western, Christian missionaries to Nigeria came to Badagry. The first sermon on Nigerian soil was preached there. The first Nigerian church, school and hospital were all built in Badagry. And the first Nigerian Bible translation in Yoruba is housed in a little museum in the city center.

Two, as previously mentioned, it is the place where over half a million enslaved were sent from the shores of West Africa. We discovered that during the slave trade, some tribal leaders of Badagry were assisting the European slave traders in order to save their own people. Because of that, the enslaved, brought to Badagry, locked in those horrific cells, then dragged away in chains and forced to lose their identity, looked back and cursed Badagry.

When we first visited the city, we asked ourselves, "What is wrong with this picture?" Locals and even some of our Imani Fellowship said Badagry was known to be cursed. There was a palatable sense of darkness and foreboding in Badagry. People talked about it, believed it, and it kept the city from significant development. Amid this darkness, we said among ourselves, if the church could come here and be the church — be salt, and light — then the darkness could be dispelled.

Our fellowship started to plan. On our collective projects, we would choose an anchor partner to oversee the project, have the most influential vote, and be responsible for its continuation. The remainder of the churches would support, contribute, and engage with the anchor partner in various ways.

March 2014, at the site of what would become the IB Transformational Engagement Center in Badagry.

Charismatic Renewal Ministries (CRM) was chosen because since 2004, they were the denomination who had focused the most on community development in several locations. They were the right group to become our first anchor partner in Badagry. Their acceptance of this request was extraordinary. CRM consists of 600+ churches, predominately from the Igbo tribe and is headquartered in eastern Nigeria, twelve hours drive from Badagry. The General Overseer is Dr. Cosmas Ilechukwu, one of our original founding members from 2004.

My dear friend and one of the Imani Bridges founders, Dr. Cosmas Ilechukwu, in 2017.

Less than fifty years earlier, the Igbo tribe suffered horribly from the Nigerian civil war, when they tried to become a new country, Biafra. In that war, the other two major tribes, the Yoruba and Hausa, sided against them. Their desire to secede was because they felt marginalized by the rest of the country and the government. This was a major reason why the war was fought. Now, in 2013, Imani Bridges was asking these leaders from CRM to anchor our new work in Badagry, a city in Yoruba land.

Once Cosmas agreed for CRM to serve in this role, he had to convince his leaders, which took some time. CRM then had to raise over $100,000 to purchase the land to build a primary school and daycare center that would also serve as a Transformational Engagement Center (TEC) where various activities can be offered year-round.

Lastly, they agreed to be responsible for the long-term sustainability of the property and programs. Cosmas assigned their missions organization, Missions Aid International (MAI), led by Emmanuel (Emmajo) Nwachukwu, to work directly with me to realize this vision. In addition to building the TEC, we decided to launch an annual, one-week mission outreach to the city.

The church in Africa must mature to the point where she would have the capacity to help the society in more practical ways than just preaching.

— Dr. Cosmas Ilechukwu

2014

I took the first Americans other than Sayres with me to Nigeria in January 2014 on a vision trip. Honestly, because of the traditional mission models that are so engrained in most Christians today, I knew bringing other Americans would quite possibly be fraught with problems.

To be sure, that first vision trip, as well as our first mission week in Badagry in March 2014, were both very turbulent. Some of the Americans I brought, as well as a few Nigerians in the Imani Fellowship, slipped into old patterns.

There were Americans who ignored the need for IB other than as an initial connector, from which they could launch their own dreams with various individual Nigerian partners. It was incredibly challenging to keep the focus on unity, our goal of collaboration, and building the strength of the body.

Despite the setbacks, some positive things happened during the March mission week. The Lord brought us a gifted Nigerian eye surgeon who held his first clinic and performed cataract surgeries. We had joyous evangelistic meetings at the town hall. The first vocational training was provided on the land purchased for the future school/daycare and TEC. But the negative issues required the next three years to work through and sort out.

The most important contribution Imani Bridges has made is building bridges across the divides. It is absolutely incredible! We have different cultures, different values, among the Nigerians and with the Americans, but we are all united in the bond of Christ. Age-long prejudices of racism, religion, tribes, power, all are separating factors. These things have been responsible for so many problems in the world and the church. Imani Bridges has given us tools to overcome these divides.

– Pastor Remi Oluboba, Provincial Pastor,
Redeemed Christian Church of God

Time To Regroup

Even though we continued building the TEC and holding some vocational training, we had no mission trips to Badagry during that time. Very few understood why, but we needed time to break down old paradigms. It took many individual meetings among the Americans and Nigerians.

I realized some of the Americans were not a good match for IB, and they were not asked to participate further. Many were unwilling to work within the collaborative, or embrace the long-term journey to develop sustainable relationships.

In Nigeria, many Imani Fellowship members were accustomed to competing for resources instead of working in unity and love for a common purpose. I spent those three years with them in prayer and Imani Fellowship meetings as we discovered how to unlearn old habits of how to interact with westerners and with each other. The Lord gave us great grace and patience during this time.

The mistakes helped us create tools for reflection and learning. 2014–2017 allowed everyone involved to step back and understand how the IB model works, what we did wrong in 2014, and what was required to launch another mission trip.

The key to a successful model of unity among a diverse group is to understand each one is a "part" and not the "it" in the room. This is counter cultural, both in America and Nigeria, and not easy for any to learn, but we created a safe place to learn together.

It also requires long-term perseverance through the hard times. Some drifted away, but most stayed, and I am content with those committed to the long haul. We continued to build deep and trusting relationships, putting aside differences, and embracing our oneness in Christ. Love and trust are two sides of a common coin.

The thing I found so compelling about Kathy is the high level of relationships she'd formed in Nigeria. My heart, like her heart, is not just for global missions, but for the Church to rise up and be the Church. It really is unique, in that Kathy has relationships at a level that even many global organizations don't have. That is, she has relationships with heads of denominations.

But this vision is held at such a high level with key leaders having bought into this paradigm and wanting their entire denomination to understand that and be practitioners of that. That is totally unique, and I've yet to see anybody else in the world doing that kind of connection and facilitation of mission through denominational leaders of many stripes, bringing them together.

– Pastor Keith Stewart, Senior Pastor, Springcreek Church

In order to launch another mission trip, preparation, training, and local organizing would be required. In 2016, the decision was made to launch the Imani Leadership Institute (ILI). The program spans three years and is comprised of six, two or three-day classes meeting semi-annually. Each class covers one aspect of the BRIDGE framework.

Most of the churches that have partnered with us and Imani Bridges, including our own church, have gone into our own communities and we're making an impact and blessing our society.

It's not about my denomination, it's about the Kingdom of God, that is what we have learnt through Imani Bridges.

— Leke Akinola, General Overseer, Upper Room Baptist Church

Teaching at the Imani Leadership Institute at Upper Room Baptist Church in Ketu, Lagos.

ILI was intended to train church leaders who are general overseers and their senior pastors, and classes are taught by both Americans and Nigerians. Leke Akinola, General Overseer of Upper Room Baptist Church was chosen to host ILI at his main campus in Ketu. He selected a group of pastors who were his peers and other church leaders to participate in the training.

In late 2016, as we planned for the re-launch of the mission week in Badagry, we knew one of our greatest challenges would be to see our vision become grassroots driven. How could we take a mission paradigm that had been caught by a diverse group of national and international Nigerian leaders and now introduce it into a particular place? The goal, though, was to incarnate it in the churches with the same diversity as we had among our national leaders. To become sustainable, these local leaders had to adopt this vision of inclusiveness and collaboration as their own.

Our first step was to gather Badagry pastors who represented the diversity of the community and attempt to create a local fellowship. The meeting included a reintroduction of Imani Bridges and vision casting. It was our desire for them to be integral in decision making.

ILI class in 2016. The program was beginning to gain momentum.

The initial meeting, held in early 2017, was attended largely by pastors who thought they could "share the goods coming from America." Some of them even asked if there was any financial benefit in the outreach for their churches. The room was full, but once it was explained that Imani Bridges was not a financial giving organization, many did not return. The second meeting of local pastors was much smaller, but these leaders were intent to learn.

This was very counter-cultural for us to ask the pastors in one of the poorest communities in Nigeria to start thinking about what they could bring and accomplish together in a city-wide mission week to meet the needs in Badagry. It was difficult for them to comprehend.

We suggested they take up offerings in their churches, however meager, offer the use of their facilities for programs, and see if they had medical professionals and others who could volunteer their time. Excitement grew as they realized their churches could contribute toward the March mission. Now with a small but committed group of local congregations, plans moved ahead for the 2017 mission outreach in Badagry.

2017

By this time, parts of the Transformational Engagement Center (TEC) buildings were built and usable. Regular vocational training was launched in 2017, with the primary school opening in 2018.

CRM and Missions Aid International (MAI), as the anchor partner in Badagry, now had the primary responsibility of completing the TEC and leading the effort for the March mission, with participation from other fellowship members.

For the weeklong outreach in Nigeria, both in 2017 and in each successive year, our Nigerian partners provided transportation, drivers, facilities throughout the city, lodging for Nigerian volunteers, and gathered volunteers from across the country who contributed to vocational training, medical assistance, and Gospel outreach. The U.S. team members also integrated with the Nigerians through vocational training, outreach and providing some financial contributions.

The first time I went, was for the mission week in 2017, the week that led up to when the Iroko tree caught fire. The favor of God on the unity expressed that week was so thickly tangible and beautiful. I've never seen anything like it. Even though there were problems that needed to be solved along the way, God's presence of blessing was so incredibly evident.

– Dr. Karissa Glanville, Author, Teacher, Speaker

Opening ceremony for the March 2017 Mission week at the Badagry Town Hall. Many Imani Bridges volunteers in their shirts are scattered throughout the crowd.

March 2017 is when the opening story for this book took place. It was an incredible week on many levels and the miracles that happened confirmed our entire journey and launched the growth of Imani Bridges onto an exponential curve.

Seventeen Americans took the journey in 2017. This group was very special because it included my son Jonathan, his future wife Cara, plus two

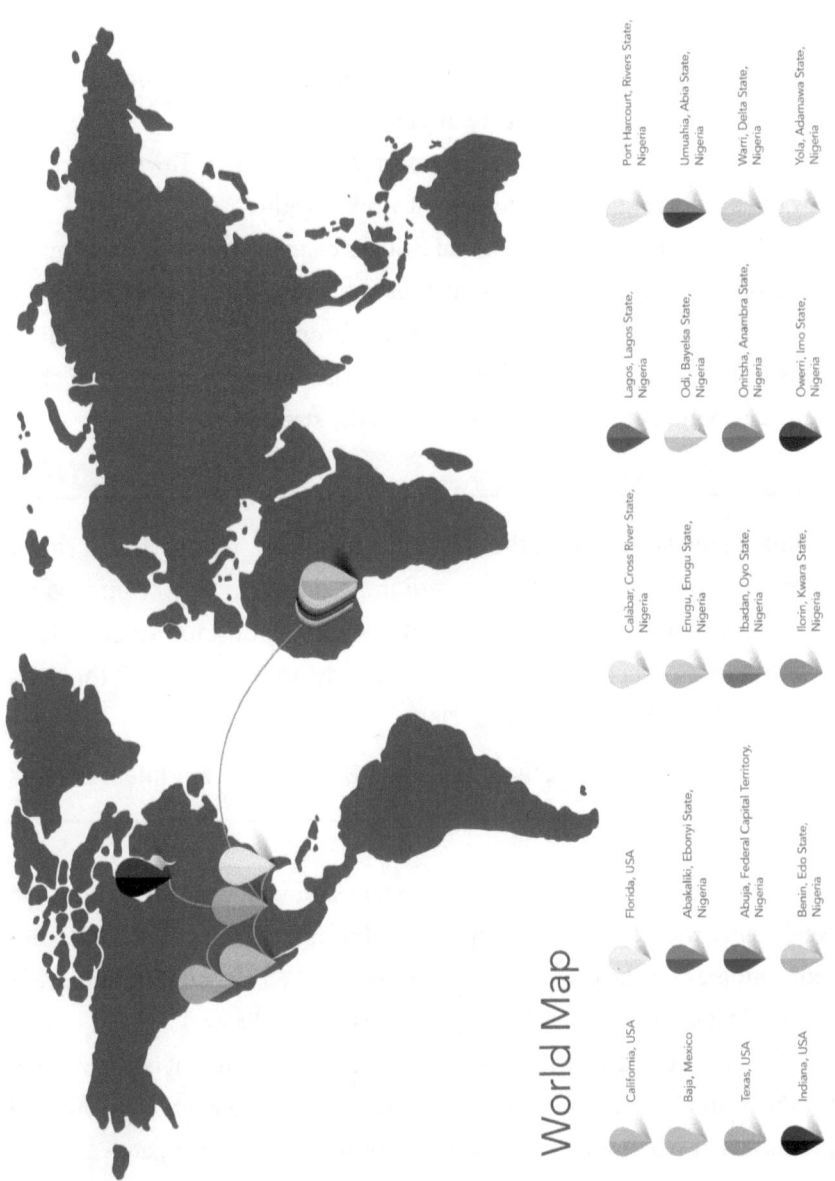

Map showing where volunteers travelled from for the 2017 Mission week.

of the Voice of Hope Promise Kids, Tonya Giraud and Jonda Mitchell. To see them as adults ministering in Nigeria filled my heart with joy.

While we were heading to Nigeria, 356 Nigerians were being mobilized — one hundred and nine from Badagry, and the rest took a two to thirteen hour drive to participate in this mission.

After an incredible opening ceremony at the Badagry Town Centre, we saw the beauty of the local churches at work together.

Many of the churches put Imani Bridges banners over their own church signs for the entire week. Some churches held evangelistic outreaches in the evening in their neighborhoods, under the banner of Imani Bridges. Nigerians and Americans, led by a brilliant Nigerian leader, teamed up for child evangelism in many of the schools and on the streets.

I think on my second trip, the mission trip in 2017, that's when it really came to light. It's a different paradigm, a different way of approaching mission, in the sense that we just want to continue to build that relationship and continue to let everybody know we're just there as another part of the Body of Christ.

– J.D. Peel, Business Owner, Board Member - Imani Bridges

There were fifteen tracks of vocational training offered throughout the week. Since the TEC wasn't completed, some of the classes were held under tent canopies on the grounds, or in almost finished classrooms. Hundreds received vital training in skills they could use immediately.

Quality medical care is a vital part of the outreach since it is out of reach for the normal citizen. Fifteen of the 356 Nigerian volunteers were medical professionals who took time off from their practice to participate.

Cataracts, a very treatable condition, are the leading cause of blindness in Nigeria. One of the doctors was an eye surgeon, Dr. Gabriel Okorodudu, from Benin City, seven hours away. Dr. Okorodudu is a wonderful example

Our American team at the airport in Brussels, half-way to Nigeria.

Original VOH Promise Kids, Tonya Giraud and Jonda Mitchell, go to Nigeria with us.

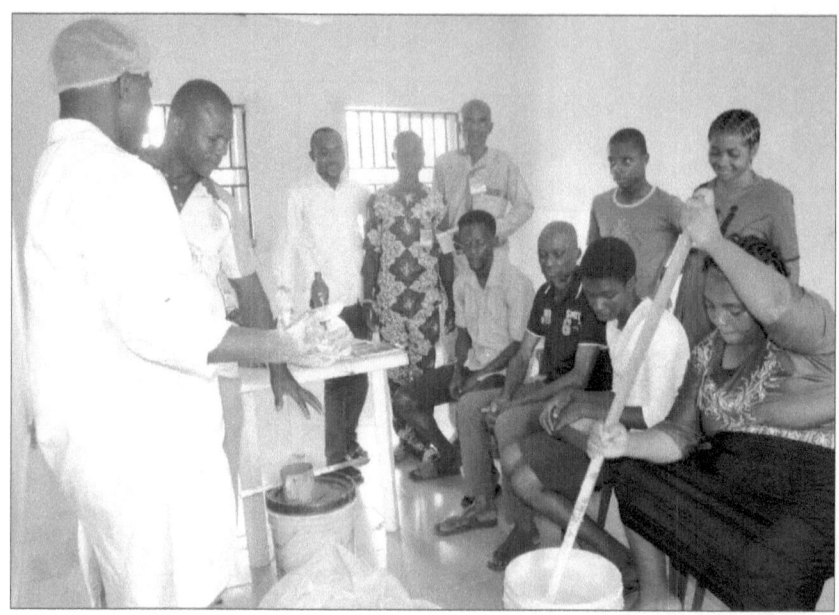

A soap making class where students learn a skill and how to start a business.

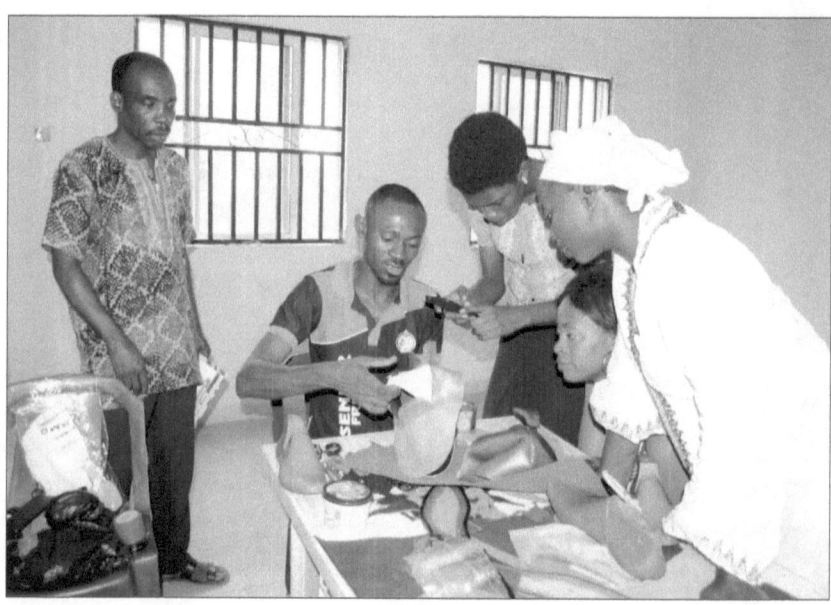

Shoe making vocational class. We observed the finished products at the closing ceremony.

of compassionate Christianity. He is Catholic, and his brother, Patrick, is a Pentecostal and Nigerian American businessman living in Indiana.

In 2014 and subsequent years, Patrick paid for his brother's medical team to travel and stay in Badagry for the outreach week, plus the expenses for most of the cataract surgeries performed. During the outreach week, the main Anglican church in Badagry offers a space in their church building for the doctor to set up a surgical suite. This beautiful picture of partnership under Imani Bridges between Catholic, Anglican, and Pentecostal brethren resulted in bringing sight to the blind in Badagry.

We learned from Dr. Okorodudu that simple cataract surgeries are crucial in Nigeria, but often unaffordable. In Nigerian culture, when someone loses their sight, they become ostracized. If a community leader goes blind, they may lose influence. Women, especially, can become beggars.

I like Imani Bridges, you spoke my language, as if we came from the same village. I came and I met Kathy, and straight out, I could tell. We did the first set of outings. I don't want to sound cliché, but she could be my sister, just that she's white. You don't find too many people like that, that you feel comradeship with. You just feel at home.

– Dr. Gabriel Okorodudu, Eye Surgeon,
Founder Africa Cataract Foundation

But imagine if a person is given the gift of sight again and can re-enter society. One woman was blind for forty years and her daughter heard about the clinic and brought her across the border from Benin. Within twenty-four hours, as the bandages came off her eyes, pure joy radiated on her face as she saw her daughter for the first time in forty years and we all wept. It is still one of the most memorable events I have ever witnessed.

Also, imagine the difference it makes when a patient receives their sight and is then introduced to the surgeon who is also Nigerian, versus seeing a

124 • BRIDGES

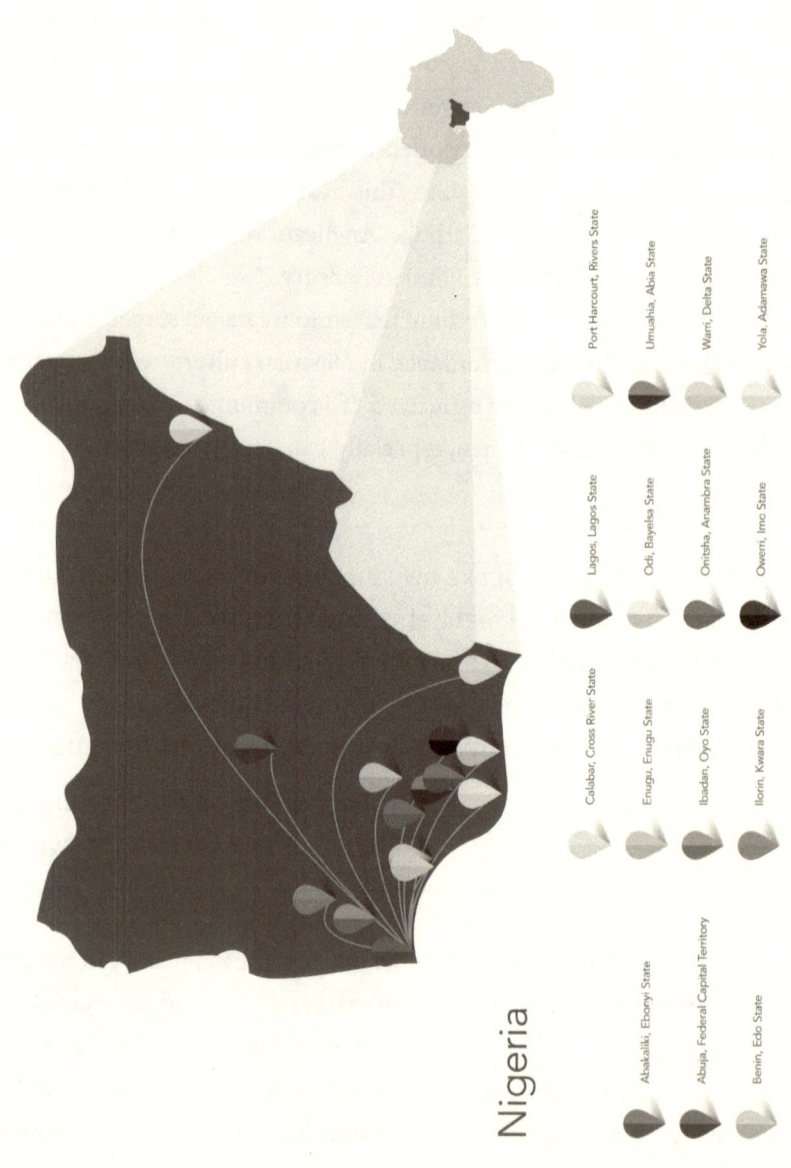

Nigeria

white doctor. Our stated mission at IB is to bring God glory and honor and esteem the local people, their culture and needs. Whatever our US team did was simply in a supporting role, to help however we could, and that has continued to the present.

At the end of the 2017 mission week, the response was incredibly positive from the churches in Badagry. The burning of the Iroko tree had caught the attention of many of the local church leaders, and they began to reconsider being involved with IB. They also saw the other fruit that had happened from that week.

As a result of the success in March, we launched a Badagry Imani Leadership Institute (ILI) in October 2017. We used both the classroom setting of ILI, and the mission week to help the local leadership understand what, how and why IB operates, and hopefully embrace the BRIDGE paradigm.

We anticipated up to thirty participants, but when we arrived in October, there were over eighty pastors/leaders who attended, hungry to know more. They understood the spiritual connections between all the events in March, including the burning of the Iroko tree.

Since 2017, the Badagry pastors/leaders have continued to come together in unity and join us in increasing number. Their enthusiasm and passion encourage us that the vision is truly taking hold at a grassroots level.

What allowed us to do this? How could a belief system and principles help make this happen? In the next section, let me introduce the BRIDGE framework.

Imani Bridges has greatly affected Badagry. People have come to Christ and grown in Christ. It has brought different churches and denominations together where we relate to one another very well. We now unite to organize programs where this was not happening before. Imani Bridges has opened our eyes to different avenues where the gospel can be preached. People have hope for living now.

– Venerable Dickson Ilegbusi, Anglican Communion, Badagry

We called her Radiant Joy as she praised God at one of the outdoor evangelism services.

This crowded room of church and pastor leaders participates in the Badagry ILI class in October 2019.

CHAPTER 11

Introduction to the BRIDGE™: A Missional Paradigm

> "When you build bridges, you can keep crossing them."
> — RICK PITINO

The "BRIDGE" is an acronym for the principles of beliefs, relationships, interdependence, development, grassroots-driven, and empowerment. These principles have been in existence since the founding of the Christian faith. The BRIDGE framework helps us see them connected, over and against our normal default system.

It represented the principles and theological belief system I had informally practiced for many years at Rhema Home Ministries and Voice of Hope. But DLF provided a perfect playground to be intentional about using the framework.

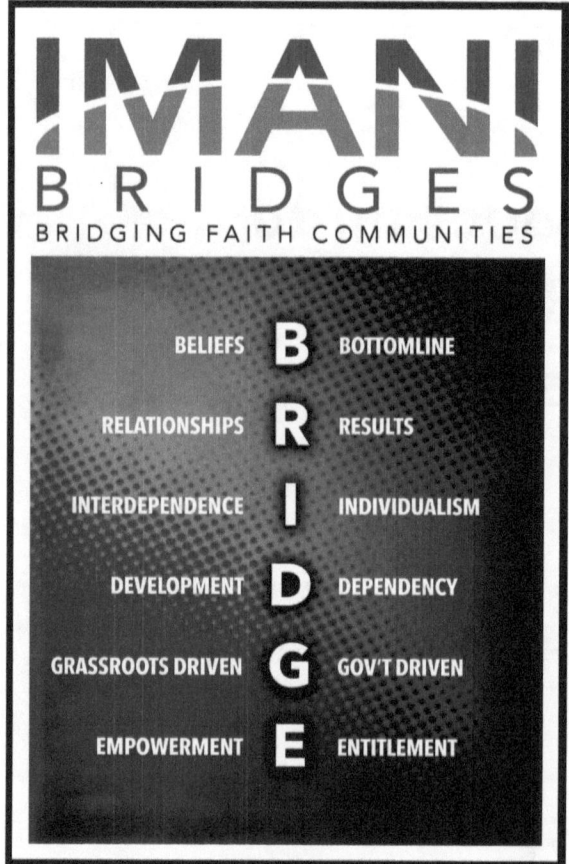

Figure 1

In the diagram, the new paradigm principles are on the left side of the word, BRIDGE. In contrast, on the right side are the modes of operation commonly used in general society. To embrace the new paradigm does not necessarily mean the principles on the right are not valuable. It is simply how they are emphasized.

It is my belief that the principles on the left, when laid on a foundation of biblical equality, far exceed those on the right in bringing fruitfulness and transformational change to the individual, church, and society. This is partly because the belief system on the left provides for full participation and a sense of "ownership" of the vision from those historically disenfranchised and marginalized in our society.

People and groups do not lose their voice when uniting under these principles. In fact, the more marginalized they are, the more their voice will be able to increase, because of the aim to balance the scales of equality. We used these principles to guide the decisions and commitments of DLF and later, Imani Bridges.

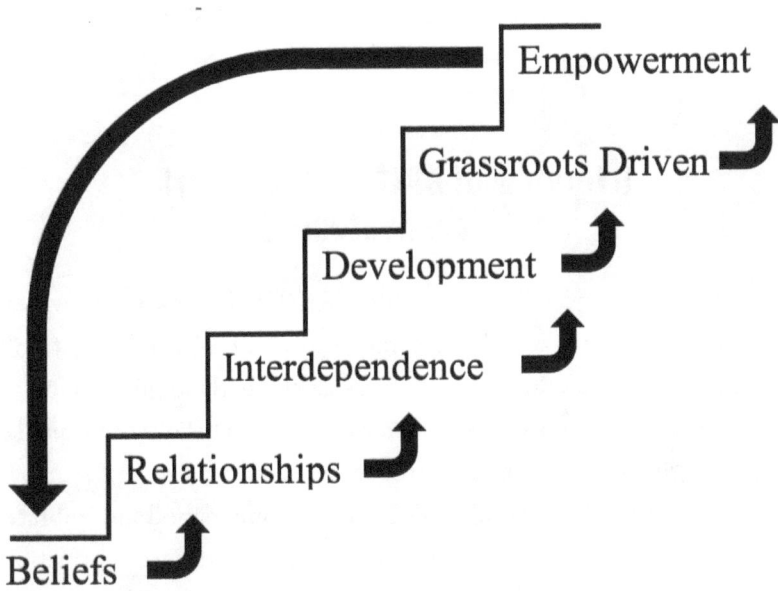

Figure 2

The BRIDGE model can be seen as a literal "bridge" that allows various people and groups to work together to bring societal transformation. It can also be seen as a staircase, that in the end, wraps back around to the beginning.

I have found the BRIDGE Framework a formidable tool for unity and justice. It is Bible-based, Spirit-driven, proven, and simple. The BRIDGE is a biblical framework for the church to bring about social change. The BRIDGE calls people to faithfulness to God and God's Word as its primary focus. It enjoins biblical definitions and applications of personal righteousness, social justice, equality, and community to bring life to communities ravaged by poverty, racism, and gender bias.

– Dr. Kwesi Kamau, Senior Pastor, Impact Church

Overview of BRIDGE Framework Interconnectedness

Built on a "theology of equality," the BRIDGE framework provides a platform for collective action. Thus, the Body of Christ can bring its gifts, callings, assets, tools, and dreams to work as one body to glorify God and transform society. The BRIDGE provides a common belief system and language to facilitate the collaborative process.

Once the principles of the BRIDGE are fully understood and embraced, the principles work in a synergistic way to activate the transformational process. It is more like six balls moving in harmony in a way that you won't even notice the individual parts. It functions as a system of core beliefs that naturally guide our actions individually and collectively.

INTRODUCTION TO THE BRIDGE™: A MISSIONAL PARADIGM • 131

The BRIDGE Framework in Action

If not for the divine arrangement that brought those bishops together that was able to bring us to where we are today in this IB platform, a lot of old beliefs probably would have stayed up where they were, and a lot of work that has been done in lives and communities may not have been possible today.

— Dr. EmmaJoe Nwachukwu, Co-Founder, Missions Aid International

---

CHAPTER 12

The BRIDGE Framework in Scripture

Though I had been discovering the principles for years at VOH and DLF, the Lord miraculously revealed the actual BRIDGE framework to me in 1996. I was to speak at a Mayor's Breakfast in the small city of Abilene, TX. The night before, my hosts in the city kept me up late into the night, touring neighborhoods and asking questions.

After returning to the hotel, I realized all my notes were at home. The Mayor's Breakfast was at six a.m. There were no previous speeches I could "pull off the shelf." Around midnight, after twenty minutes of fretting, I said, "Lord, please don't embarrass Yourself or me tomorrow. Give me something that's meaningful," and I fell sleep.

About an hour later, I literally sat straight up in the bed, and the BRIDGE framework came to me like a revelation. I sensed the Lord was saying, "Most people operate on the right side of this paradigm. You have been operating on the left side, but did not have a language for it."

I drew this diagram on a marker board and explained it at the breakfast that morning and since then, at countless meetings. Before I shared it broadly, however, I needed to explore the theology behind it, as it required

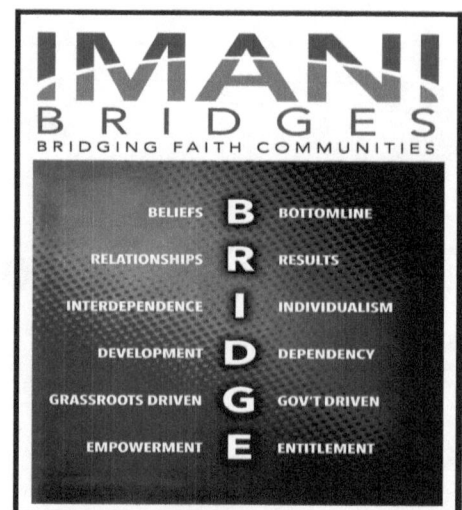

The BRIDGE Framework

a biblical context. My study led me to key Scriptures, and it became apparent the framework and related Scriptures were like a bridge. Focusing on key Scriptures (covered below), gives us the foundational beliefs required to answer the prayer of Jesus, starting with an understanding of the Lord's prayer (Matthew 6:9-15).

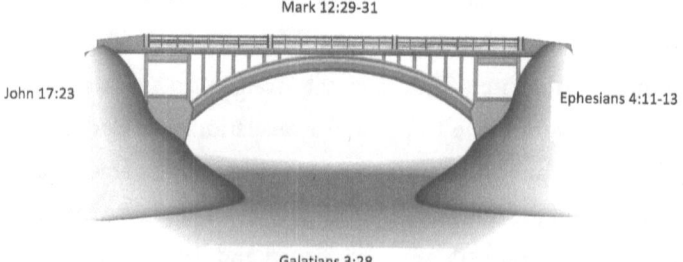

Here, Jesus tells us to pray that "His kingdom come" and "His will be done on earth as it is in heaven." This is God's purpose and mission for His people. We, as His body, are His hands and feet to carry out His purpose in the world. This verse provides the backdrop for all our activity.

We've already looked at John 17:23, the prayer of Jesus for His disciples then and now. That verse is an anchor of the bridge. This is God Himself, in the flesh, praying for us. We know it's important and relates to *us* because He says, "I'm praying for you, and those who will come after you." Believers everywhere, from Catholics to Pentecostals, should agree that this prayer of Jesus is important, and one God expects us to answer.

Another anchor passage of Scripture is Ephesians 4. Here, Paul emphasizes there is one God and one church. He goes on to say, Christ has given a gift to the church, the gift of Apostles, Prophets, Evangelists, Pastors, and Teachers. Why? "To equip the saints for the work of the ministry" (Ephesians 4:12). Every believer sitting in the church is meant to be equipped for ministry, regardless of their vocation, profession, or location, as they represent all sectors of society.

I still wondered though, what was the overarching concept that connected everything? Jesus gave us the secret in Mark 12:29-31. "Hear oh Israel: The Lord our God, the Lord is one. Love the Lord your God with all your heart and with all your soul and with all your mind and with all your strength." Then He said, "The second is this, Love your neighbor as yourself. There is no commandment greater than these."

It sounds simple, love God and love others. But how do we love God, ourselves, and others out of the love God has for us? The secret is right there in the verse — with all our heart, all our soul, all our mind, all our strength.

This means that when I get up each morning and go for my usual walk and time to pray, I am not just loving God by being spiritual, I am loving God because I am also exercising my body, the temple of the Holy Spirit (1 Corinthians 6:19).

Let me extend this thought into practical application. If we provide ministry in healthcare, education, clean water, evangelism, vocational training, etc., we are loving God and others by dealing holistically with God's creation and with people. We walk in love as the people of God with all our heart, soul, mind, and strength.

Empowering people must begin with helping them discover that their human dignity and identity are intrinsically related to God in Christ through His redemptive purpose and not in any of the world's biased categories. One cannot imagine the positive revolution this view of ministry will generate in Africa when the people in the church begin to see their routine jobs and businesses as legitimate ministries to God. There can be no better way to empower the people for transformation of their communities.

– Dr. Cosmas Ilechukwu

For me, what undergirds our ability to obey and fulfill Mark 12:29 is a foundational belief in the theology of equality. Do we honestly see others as equals at the foot of the Cross, regardless of race, culture, gender, economic status, theological or political beliefs?

In Galatia, Paul was challenged to create a unified body from a very diverse group of people: Jews and Gentiles, Romans and Greeks, wealthy and poor, free people and slaves, men and women. This was a society where these differences were magnified, but Paul said, "So in Christ Jesus you are all children of God through faith" (Galatians 3:26). Then he gave his cornerstone verse:

> *"There is neither Jew nor Gentile,*
> *neither slave nor free,*
> *neither male nor female,*
> *for you are all one in Christ Jesus."*
> Galatians 3:28

My belief in oneness and equality permeates every facet of my life, relationships, and ministry. It is the lens through which I view everyone.

Let me explore this verse for a moment. What is today's equivalent of saying there is no Jew or Gentile in Christ? In America, we would say racism does not exist; in Nigeria, no tribalism. No slave nor free in Christ would translate, classism is non-existent. No male nor female in Christ is simple; sexism is eliminated. Let's be honest though. We all know this is not the reality in the Body of Christ, but this should not discourage us from remembering that "if anyone is in Christ, the new creation has come: The old is gone, the new is here" (2 Corinthians 5:17).

I believe these three *isms* (racism, classism, and sexism) are at the root of most problems today, in and outside of the church. I shared these teachings with the Bishop's class in 2004. These men came from a wide difference in tribal backgrounds, belief systems, church denominations and cultural norms, yet the Holy Spirit unified them in understanding this fundamental truth of oneness and equality.

When we discuss the issue of interdependence, one thing that came out very strongly was the issue of being able to give the wives an opportunity to play a role in the great harvest, and not just be the kitchen people. Praise the Lord. This was something that was controversial, but we were bold to discuss it. And I know a lot of homes that were turned around because of it. People called me and said to me, "Look, I have found my wife is alive again!"

– Dr. Nkem Nwachukwu, Co-Founder, Missions Aid International

This is how Imani Bridges was born, centered on this understanding to answer the prayer of Jesus. This theology of equality gave myself and the bishops the platform and ability to navigate our journey, and it allowed me to lead in a way that insisted on equality, especially since I was a female.

One of my favorite examples of the outworking of the theology of equality concerns a Nigerian named Ovie Godfrey. Ovie, though college educated, had like so many Nigerians in their difficult economy, fallen on hard times and was now working as a driver. He was one of the van drivers for our American team members during the March 2017 outreach. In Nigeria, a driver is often considered a lowly person, not one to command respect. One of our team members, Dr. Betsy Glanville, a retired professor from Fuller Seminary, truly connected with Ovie. She would always hurry to take the front passenger seat next to him, and after a few times, he would save the seat for her.

As I sat and watched this beautiful scene, I wondered, how could this be? Betsy is an older, educated, white American woman who has taught and mentored doctoral students around the world, and here she is with her new friend, Ovie.

Every day that week, the American team had morning and evening devotions, joined by Nigerian partners. We invited our drivers to join us, a total paradigm shift in that society. One evening, Ovie stood up, with Nigerian leaders all around him, but he was not intimidated. He talked about observations and new knowledge, how important it was, and his contribution to the discussion was beautiful. That is how the BRIDGE framework impacts relationships.

The following year, just before our return, someone tried to steal Ovie's car and in the scuffle, killed our dear friend. It was devastating, as we had all come to love Ovie deeply. However, his story did not end with his death.

His church, Upper Room Baptist, is one of our anchor partners. In 2019, Imani Bridges launched a solar energy school at Upper Room. We had decided to start a scholarship program for this school and other vocational training programs. Both Nigerians and Americans agreed it should be named after him.

When I spoke to the Upper Room congregation and announced the Ovie Godfrey scholarship, at first the congregants were puzzled and silent.

Suddenly, everyone rose to their feet with thunderous applause and shouts. In addition to being a driver, Ovie was a small group leader and was involved in ministry throughout the church. We learned he was beloved and greatly missed.

This was the evidence of fruit in a long process, one where a theology of equality had taken root, even when it was counter cultural. Our joy continued, as after the church service, Betsy learned Ovie's widow was interested in attending the solar training program. She immediately agreed to sponsor her and she became the first recipient of the scholarship.

This story is one example of the BRIDGE framework in action; based firmly on Scripture and a theology of equality. The next chapters provide a deeper look at the significance of the theology, and examples of each principle of the model.

One of the most thrilling parts of all my trips to Nigeria has been seeing the increasing unity among all those involved. The original bishops have such a unique bond of love and respect for one another and for Kathy and all the Imani team. I see that same commitment growing among the pastors and leaders in Badagry, as they work together.

— Dr. Betsy Glanville, Senior Affiliate Faculty,
Fuller School of Mission and Theology

CHAPTER 13

The BRIDGE Framework Principles Part One

Beliefs

"So in Christ Jesus you are all children of God through faith, for all of you who were baptized into Christ have clothed yourselves with Christ. There is neither Jew nor Gentile, neither slave nor free, neither male nor female, for you are all one in Christ Jesus."
Galatians 3:26-28

The theology of equality discussed above is the perfect example of the power and importance of beliefs. Beliefs form the very foundation of our theology and affect everything in our lives. To know what one believes, just look at how they prioritize their time, talent, and resources. It is not what we say, but how we live that reveals our deepest beliefs and values.

In the context of Galatians 3:26-28, Paul is describing the freedom brought by the Gospel. The fact that he places equality squarely in his description of, and argument for, the freedom found in the Gospel, is significant. The foundation of this framework, and everything else built upon it, are biblical principles which include a theology of equality.

I believe when equality is a lens through which we view others, we can then honor and learn from one another, and share power. On the other hand, if we believe in class structures and gender inequality, our practices will denote hierarchy or patriarchy. Equality insists on respect, mutuality, integrity, humility, and vulnerability.

Equality does not mean "sameness." The unique history, setting, context, gifts, and perspectives of everyone are honored and weighed in each situation. Each setting though, is unique. What we do in Nigeria is contextualized for that setting and looks very different from what we have done in Dallas. However, the general expressions of progress toward transformation are similar: people, neighborhoods and churches are all being transformed.

> *The eye cannot say to the hand, "I don't need you!" And the head cannot say to the feet, "I don't need you!" On the contrary, those parts of the body that seem to be weaker are indispensable, and the parts that we think less honorable we treat with special honor. And the parts that are unpresentable are treated with special modesty, while our presentable parts need no special treatment. But God has put the body together, giving greater honor to the parts that lacked it, so that there should be no division in the body, but that its parts should have equal concern for each other.*
> I C orinthians 12: 21-25

Examples

No matter the context, the scales of injustice can be equalized by adhering to principles such as "the partner who is closest to the problem has the greater authority." In Dallas, the neighborhood leaders chose who received benefits in our collaborative efforts of neighborhood revitalization. The community partners had a greater voice on decisions that were made, and the leadership in each project was chosen first from among the community sponsors and partners.

In Badagry, Nigeria, the local anchor partners selected the project which the other fellowship members joined in to complete. Now there is an elected leadership team to represent the local Badagry Imani Fellowship.

In Dallas, church partners played different roles based on their "closeness to the problem." The community church might be a "local partner" in the neighborhood in which it is located, and only be a "supporting partner" in another community. Likewise, in Nigeria, there are local "anchor partners" and broader members of the "Fellowship." These arrangements allow the practice of mutual submission and respect of the grassroots partners, regardless of race, location, tribe, or socioeconomic status.

Even partners who espouse a hierarchical theology and model of Christian leadership are attracted to and have participated in our projects. Through modeling this genuine belief in, and practice of equality, room is made for everyone, providing a safe place to learn, work and grow. This is a core belief and value of Imani Bridges, and we constantly emphasize it for growth of our collective efforts, without which we will not be able to reach full unity or maturity.

> "The greatest need we have is not to do things, but to believe things."
> — OSWALD CHAMBERS

> "Don't walk in front of me, I may not follow.
> Don't walk behind me, I may not lead.
> Walk beside me and be my friend."
> — ALBERT CAMUS

Relationships

"Of all the commandments, which is the most important?"

"The most important one," answered Jesus, "is this. 'Hear, O Israel, the Lord our God, the Lord is one. Love the Lord your God with all your heart and with all your soul and with all your mind and with all your strength. The second is this: Love your neighbor as yourself. There is no commandment greater than these."

Mark 12:28b-31

We all want our efforts to be profitable, but if we look for quick success in numbers, programs offered, or even what the general populous expects us to do (i.e., the bottom line), we are measuring the wrong thing. Relationships built on trust and respect produce a growing environment that empowers the individual and the community to move toward transformational change.

In the end, we all want to get to the "bottom line," but at what cost? What are the outcomes? By prioritizing the theological principles in the BRIDGE framework, we accomplish more than could be imagined.

DLF and IB both had to build structures that valued relationships more than results.

Dallas

With DLF, as mentioned in a previous chapter, it was largely my values concerning relationships that led me to replace the board members. I valued a thoughtful process that would listen to the "felt needs" of people across the city. My hope and desire was to identify a common vision all could agree on and only accomplish if we worked on it together. This required strategically building significant, one-on-one relationships with key leaders who emerged in the process of listening to a diverse group of people throughout the city.

I had asked the question, "Who is respected most by those whom God has called me to serve?" As the leaders were identified, I knew God's people and resources could be unleashed for action to produce results. These "bridges of trust" were essential if our vision of Dallas becoming a city of hope for all its people, and a place where God is glorified, was to be realized.

This was a long process and proved to appear ineffective to my initial board. The new board leadership was comprised of representatives from the core church partners of DLF. I strategically chose people who were committed to the belief of equality, so the foundation of DLF would experience as little unnecessary conflict as possible.

Our belief in the power of relationships based on equality, interdependence and mutual understanding was essential in making this transition. We built bridges of hope among people and churches and neighborhoods and the city as a whole. When that happens, and the Lord is in the center of it, nearly anything can be done.

Nigeria

As with Dallas, it took years in Nigeria to build relationships and trust between myself and the leaders, and for the leaders to trust each other, starting in 2004. I mentioned earlier that these men, though students together in these week-long intensive classes over three years, had not developed personal relationships. God used my weakness with their names to break down those denominational and cultural walls and create a very different atmosphere in the room.

It wasn't until 2013 that we were challenged once again to answer the prayer of Jesus and work together in unity for a common purpose. Our relationships and trust were strong; we were now ready to embark on projects together. They had been implementing the principles in their own communities and churches, but now it was time to work collectively.

Working together in equality and unity does not mean losing one's uniqueness or calling; on the contrary, it allows each part of the body to shine in their strengths. It is my contention that if **B**eliefs do not have equality at their core, and thus woven into **R**elationships from the beginning, it will be difficult to have legitimate **I**nterdependence.

> "If broken relationships are tolerated, the body cannot build itself up in love. I look at a church's capacity for healthy relationships. The power of a church will be found in the capacity generated by healthy relationships. As relationships increase, the level of change diminishes or the resistance to it changes."
>
> — WAYNE CORDEIRO, senior pastor of New Hope Christian Fellowship in Honolulu

> "It is a deficient, unbiblical philosophy of ministry that depersonalizes ministry by valuing increased numbers over intimate relationships, programs over people, and leadership by a professional clergy over the priesthood of believers."
>
> —JOHN ROWELL

Africans lead a community-based life, which also allows for distinct social boundaries according to wealth, gender, age, grade, and titles held in the society. Family ties and tribal bonds are quite strong among Africans. However, the relationship advanced by the "bridge" paradigm transcends families, tribes, and tongues (a relationship based on equality of all people, races, and nations.

– Dr. Cosmas Ilechukwu

Interdependence

Ephesians 4:14-16 "Then we will no longer be infants, tossed back and forth by the waves, and blown here and there by every wind of teaching and by the cunning and craftiness of people in their deceitful scheming. Instead, speaking the truth in love, we will in all things grow up into him who is the head, that is, Christ. From him the whole body, joined and held together by every supporting ligament, grows, and builds itself up in love, as each part does its work."

Romans 12: 4-5 "For just as each of us has one body with many members, and these members do not all have the same function, so in Christ we, though many, form one body and each member belongs to all the others."

I Corinthians 12:12-13 "Just as a body, though one, has many parts, but all its many parts form one body, so it is with Christ. For we were all baptized by one Spirit so as to form one body — whether Jews or Gentiles, slave or free — and we were all given the one Spirit to drink."

Stephen Covey made the word interdependence famous in his best seller *The Seven Habits of Effective People,* but it was God's idea long before it was his. If there is one thing I have learned over the years, it is the importance of the Body of Christ. God has determined to work in and through His Body to display and reveal His Kingdom. This has meant a deeper understanding of both my gifts and my limitations.

As I have discovered in working in collaboration with numerous people through the years, one thing is very clear: we need one another. Each of us plays a valuable role to accomplish God's purpose on earth, the redemption of humankind. For that to happen, individualism must be replaced with a deeper understanding of interdependence. This will require a mindset change. We are so programmed to act in our own self-interest, but to be interdependent likely involves pain and sacrifice. I am convinced it is worth it.

We can overcome the inconveniences interdependence may occasion from time to time if we remember that Christ died to make us one.

– Dr. Cosmas Ilechukwu

Dallas

When I reflect on the seven years I led DLF, and acknowledge the amazing results accomplished through the unity of the Body of Christ in Dallas, I am truly amazed. By recognizing and affirming the unique gifts of individuals, churches, and sectors in society, we saw major changes. Several neighborhoods were redeveloped (four extensively), and eight new Christian non-profits were established that operate independently yet are connected relationally for city-wide initiatives. Two hundred plus businesses contributed to our efforts.

Approximately fifty churches, non-profits, and networks (such as the African American Pastors' Coalition, North Texas Conference of the United Methodist Church, and the Dallas Baptist Association) collaborated on educational programs, community development projects, Christmas initiatives and prison aftercare. We began to see the effectiveness of God's strategy of unity and oneness.

One example was seen when DLF acted as the local organizing host for the Christian Community Development Association's (CCDA) annual conference in the fall of 2001, with almost two thousand registered attendees and over 1200 coming to special events sponsored by the local CCDA Host Committee.

From October 2000, the Dallas team busily prepared for the conference with great confidence and anticipation. We were confident because our Dallas network of partners was vast and strong. As we contemplated the theme, nothing seemed more appropriate than the phrase "Come Together." However, little did we realize how much we would need to work together, grow together, struggle together, cry together and love together to prove our unity. Our commitment to oneness was tested in ways that none of us could have foreseen.

Our co-host, Rev. Dr. E. K. Bailey suddenly faced health challenges that ultimately took his life. The U.S. economy failed in the first quarter of 2001. The NAACP boycotted the Adam's Mark Hotel where the conference was slated to be held, thus a venue change was required. Our country was attacked on 9/11, we went to war and air travel was changed forever.

Yet in all this, the church in Dallas was victorious in proving how deeply committed we were to *one another*. The greatest proof that we knew how to Come Together was in our ability to stand together despite adversity.

The Church in Dallas realized the value and the need of understanding this core belief that interdependence is the way to multiplication. We see clearly in the book of Acts the value placed on unity, with tangible outward expressions of love for the poor and vulnerable.

> *"All the believers were together and had everything in common. They sold property and possessions to give to anyone who had need."*
> Acts 2:44-45

The old African proverb, "It takes a whole village to raise a child," is also a beautiful expression of this truth.

Nigeria

In Nigeria, churches have historically been as divided as they are in the U.S. However, through Imani Bridges, we have begun to see just how wonderful it is when the church works together. Below is a reflection from the perspective of Dr. Emanuel Nwachukwu, with MAI. Here, he reflects in a conversation we had on the significance of relationships and interdependence.

> Instead of individualism, relationship came in and we saw that in God's paradigm, which is Imani Bridges' paradigm, nobody is expected to be an island. There must be a reason why Jesus sent them out two by two instead of one by one. There must be a reason why Jesus wanted His work to be done this way. And we've got to learn that it's not about how much results you can make on your

own. But that when you learn to relate across the board, you will find that giftings are different.

You will find you will learn from our brother or sister across the divide. We also learn from our brothers and sisters who are coming from America. And they are also learning from us at the same time. There is everything to benefit and nothing to lose.

The one that shocked me most, our denomination came out of the Catholic Church, so we had an attitude to Catholics that is, how to say, condescending. Through IB, we also came across Catholics, and it's like, "Wow! What is different between us and these guys?" So, some form of respect came in the change in beliefs, and enhanced relationships, even with the Catholics.

Then from that individualistic attitude that we came up with, we learnt God would also have us be interdependent. There is something God has gifted me with, and there is something He has gifted you with. And I can depend on you for what you have.

This is a beautiful reflection of the relational paradigm shift seen among many pastors, leaders, and church members in Nigeria. This level of interdependence leads us to the ability to do development.

"You do not get harmony when everybody sings the same note."

— DOUG FLOYD

"Long ago, the Native Americans of the Great Plains survived the harsh winters by having grandparents and grandchildren sleep beside each other to keep from freezing to death. That is a good metaphor for what the generations do for each other. The old need our heat, and we need their light."

— MARY PIPHER

CHAPTER 14

The BRIDGE Framework Principles Part Two

Development

One day Jesus was teaching, and Pharisees and teachers of the law were sitting there. They had come from every village of Galilee and from Judea and Jerusalem. And the power of the Lord was with Jesus to heal the sick. Some men came carrying a paralyzed man on a mat and tried to take him into the house to lay him before Jesus. When they could not find a way to do this because of the crowd, they went up on the roof and lowered him on his mat through the tiles into the middle of the crowd, right in front of Jesus. When Jesus saw their faith, he said, "Friend, your sins are forgiven." The Pharisees and the teachers of the law began thinking to themselves, "Who is this fellow who speaks blasphemy? Who can forgive sins but God alone?" Jesus knew what they were thinking and asked, "Why are you thinking these things in your hearts? Which is easier to say, 'Your sins are forgiven' or to say, 'Get up and walk'? But I want you to know that the Son of Man has authority on earth to forgive sins . . . " So he said to the paralyzed man, "I tell you, get up, take your mat and go home." Immediately he stood up in from of them, took what he had been lying on and went home praising God. Everyone was amazed and gave praise to God. They were filled with awe and said, "We have seen remarkable things today."   Luke 5:17-26

This Scripture beautifully illustrates the dependence of the paralytic and the interdependence of his friends. Each friend had to carry the weight of his corner of the blanket to accomplish the job. I can imagine the determination, perseverance, and teamwork it required.

The paralytic reminds us that there are times in all our lives when we are dependent. However, in all parts of our lives, we want to move from dependency to development. Our organizational programs must also be designed with this in mind. Too often, programs for the needy are structured in a way that keeps the recipients from attaining the knowledge and tools for self-determination.

The word development means to build up, grow, or improve gradually over time. The goal of Christian community development is to work alongside individuals and communities to create positive change that occurs in the whole of human life: mentally, socially, and spiritually.

Dallas

At DLF, we valued development of the individual and the organizations we partnered with. This was seen in the number of non-profits DLF helped establish. Some of them required an incubation period and others did not. In either case, providing the connections, resources and learning experiences for continued growth was a priority.

Socially, people have been elevated from poverty. Others who were sick and had no hope of healing have received help. People have received their sight back from blindness and that has changed their lives. Imani Bridges brought in classes where people learned handiwork and now can depend on themselves to make money and feed their families. The standard of living has increased because of this.

– Venerable Dickson Ilegbusi, Anglican Communion, Badagry

One leader, whom we helped start a Christian ministry for children and youth stated, "DLF helped me find my purpose in life when no one else would give me the time or thought of a fleeting moment." This African American leader became one of our best examples of urban ministry in the city. Valuing risk often leads to the greatest victories.

True development requires a holistic approach, and most learning is incremental and built upon a little at a time. I have used the following learning model for many years and found it most effective.

>I do, you watch.
>I do, you help.
>You do, I help.
>You do, I watch.

DLF measured its effectiveness in all our relationships, programs, and events by the growth of the individuals and organizations in which we were involved. In a survey we did near the end of my time with DLF, a diverse representation of our partners said they had grown spiritually since being involved with DLF, and that this spiritual growth was a primary reason for the overall growth.

Learning and growth do not take place in a vacuum. When trying to effect change at both an individual and institutional level, different pictures and models must be provided of what *can* be, as reinforcement. At DLF, we realized painting the right picture from the beginning could accelerate the learning process.

An illustration of this could be seen in the design of the DLF office space. We wanted our space to be a learning environment that taught the important values and beliefs of the organization. One could discern our values simply by entering our office.

Our goal was to counter many of the preconceived ideas and beliefs about the African American male, therefore, the first thing visible when entering the DLF office was a statue of an African American man holding a child. We valued the Word of God and prayer, so there was a framed copy of The Lord's Prayer on the wall to the right. There was a picture of children from around the world on another wall to show our high value for children.

A map of the Dallas area spanned a wall of the conference room, because of our value for the city. We valued the church, so this also was reflected in the décor of the office. History was valued, with awards of past accomplishments displayed. We valued accountability, so a certificate revealing our membership in the Evangelical Council for Financial Accountability (ECFA) was prominently placed.

Numerous people commented on the impact of their first visit to DLF. Many minorities made the commitment to be involved simply because they could quickly assess and resonate with our beliefs and values.

Christianity is a "see and touch" Gospel. Like the Apostle John, who said, "that which we have heard, which we have seen with our eyes, which we have looked at and our hands have touched — this we proclaim concerning the Word of life" (I John 1:1). It's important to use methods that employ all the senses to teach what we believe.

Nigeria

Bishop Sam gave a beautiful example of development versus dependency at work in his church. There was a single mother in his church whose husband had left her. Sam thought she was headed towards becoming a burden to the church. He inquired how much money she would need to start her own business. She requested a moderate sum, to which he added a bit more.

It wasn't long before her small business turned a profit. He regularly checked in with her for accountability. She quickly multiplied the money ten times and asked for help to open a savings account. The church also assisted her children with education costs, but besides that, the woman became self-supporting, and is now a tither in the church.

Sam could have simply tried to meet her immediate needs, but this would have created continual dependence. Instead, he worked with her, and kept her accountable to develop her gifts and strengths. Instead of a burden, she is a blessing.

"The role of the leader is made legitimate and powerful, if recognized leaders make their followers into leaders."

— inspired by JAMES MACGREGOR BURNS

"Take chances. Make mistakes. That's how you grow. Pain nourishes your courage. You have to fail to practice being brave."

— MARY TYLER MOORE

"Individuals who are allowed to compartmentalize their convictions find that only a very private part of their lives is affected by their faith."

— JOHN ROWELL

Grassroots Driven

When Jesus had finished saying all this to the people who were listening, he entered Capernaum. There a centurion's servant, whom his master valued highly, was sick and about to die. The centurion heard of Jesus and sent some elders of the Jews to him, asking him to come and heal his servant. When they came to Jesus, they pleaded earnestly with him, "This man deserves to have you do this, because he loves our nation and has built our synagogue. So Jesus went with them. Luke 7:1-6

The Lord used this Scripture to show me the importance of respecting and honoring the culture and the leaders within the community I was called to serve. The centurion is a great example of a leader who understood authority. He was humble and obviously respectful.

First off, the elders of the Jews responded to the centurion's request. Their reasoning to Jesus was simple: "This man deserves to have you do this, because he loves our nation, and he built our synagogue." The centurion had gained the respect of the Jewish elders because he cared about the people and respected its leaders and culture.

For a strategy to be defined as grassroots driven, those closest to the problems must be recognized and engaged from the beginning as major stakeholders in the work.

Dallas

Wil McCall, an African American, succeeded me as President of DLF. He wrote to me once and said, "Because you have demonstrated that you honor people that look like me, you've made it easier to honor people that look like you." The way we reach the grassroots is by respecting the leaders they have already chosen.

DLF had a four-member staff during my tenure. DLF served as a platform for churches, non-profits, and other agencies to collaborate and work toward collective action to meet the spiritual, physical, and economic needs in Dallas communities.

Each program or partnership was delineated by elaborate organizational charts. The charts outlined duties and responsibilities, clearly defining the roles each partner in any project had agreed to assume.

A typical chart started with DLF, and flowed to the supporting partners — the churches, non-profit agencies, or organizations sponsoring a given event or activity. Community and participating partners were added. Each set of partners brought its own cluster of volunteers. Grassroots takes on a new meaning as each part of the body is expected to connect and link its vital resources to the whole.

A fun example of the power of grassroots organizing and strategic partnership happened when the Celebration of Hope Committee agreed to put in a basketball court and landscaping in one of the city parks in the neighborhood. The park was not properly cared for and was a hangout for alcoholics and drug users. The committee decided we would proceed with our plans without asking the City of Dallas for permission. Instead, we would ask for forgiveness if we got caught!

We arranged for the subcontractors to deliver their materials and begin work. On the first day of operation, a city official arrived. He asked one of our business volunteers who had authorized them to pour the concrete.

His response was, "First, you need to check with the pastor at the church down the street, Rev. Zan Holmes, because he approved it. Then check with the neighborhood leaders; they are also fully involved. Highland Park Presbyterian, Park Cities Presbyterian, Friendship West Baptist are partners in the project. My company, Hawkins-Welwood agreed to participate also, and Dallas Leadership Foundation is the organization that brought us together."

The inspector left, saying he would get back with us. It has been two and a half decades now, and we have not heard back from them. The park became an added asset to the community, and the city even takes care of it.

Praise God, I believe in the need for government action and involvement. The state is a God-given institution that plays a critical role in society. However, I believe transformational change is something that takes place in the heart. We must move from people being told they "have to," to people actually saying they "want to." Again, I quote Wil McCall from a letter he wrote to me.

> Because I have been able to work with you and learn from you, I have a number of new "want to's." I "want to" be a part of making Dallas a "city of hope." I "want to" do my part in connecting the Body of Christ in a healthy way. I "want to" promote egalitarianism. I "want to" make sure you know how much the picture of your life has influenced for the better, my perspective of the world and the church.

Nigeria

Dr. Emmanuel Nwachukwu gave the following example of how the emphasis on grassroots has been seen in IB's work in Nigeria.

We learnt from IB, that this work is not about others bringing the resources and letting us do the work. Before, we always looked out for who will bring the resources. Then we would do the work. But we learnt that the resources are in the pockets of the grassroots people. God did not put some multi-millionaires and tell them to bring the money for you. But if you are a person of faith, and you look up to God, you will find the money for the work in the mouth of the next fish. That is the grassroots. Many of us always believed that the work cannot be done because it is people distant from here who will bring the money.

When we were working in Badagry, and Kathy came up with the idea of getting the [local] churches to raise money, I laughed.

I said, "Which churches?"

And she said, "To expect them to give is a form of respect and helps them own the work. And when you're talking about money for ministry, it's not about how much. What we are looking for is commitment. Once you are committed to the work, God sends the resources."

So, we let the Badagry churches raise money in different churches. And it produced excitement! We saw the people at the opening ceremony had people from each church who would come with their envelope and give their offering. We called it Compassion Offering. They would come with their envelopes; church after church were bringing small-small money; 2,000, 5,000, 3,500 Naira [$5–10 US]. They understood this is their thing. This is their work. This is their commitment. It helped them own the work. Everybody has a part to play.

And the paradigm that America brings the money so we can work has been broken. Today, when we want to work, we look for the money among us. They [Americans] can bring the money as they also look for the money over there, but we don't look across the ocean for the money; the money is here. So that lesson can be taken back to our churches. The money for the work of God is in your pockets. It's in the pockets of the people. Don't think they are poor because they are not.

> "Your success will be determined by how many other people you help to become more successful."
>
> — BILLY HORNSBY

> "When you dig another out of their troubles, you find a place to bury your own."
>
> — ANONYMOUS

> "God chose to make fig pickers into prophets, prisoners into prime ministers, little Jewish girls into queens, shepherd boys into giant killers and kings, and common fisherman into founders of His church."
>
> — JOHN ROWELL

Empowerment

Jesus knew that the Father had put all things under his power, and that he had come from God and was returning to God, so he got up from the meal, took off his outer clothing, and wrapped a towel around his waist. After that, he poured water into a basin and began to wash his disciples' feet, drying them with the towel that was wrapped around him… When he had finished washing their feet, he put on his clothes and returned to his place. "Do you understand what I have done for you?" he asked them. "You call me 'Teacher' and 'Lord', and rightly so, for that is what I am. Now that I, your Lord and Teacher, have washed your feet, I have set you an example that you should do as I have done for you." John 13:3-4;13-14

Jesus was saying, I know who I am, and it is because of this that I can show you the full extent of my love. It is because of this that I can serve you.

This understanding of servanthood has been one of the most important lessons in my life. First, it is out of knowing who we are in Christ that we can truly love and serve. *It is not what we do, but who we are.* That is where the power comes from. Second, as we serve others, God makes room for our gifts and we are empowered by others to be used for His glory.

Everything in this BRIDGE framework moves toward mutual respect, unity, and equality. It is unity that leads to transformation, both personal and societal. We have found that these principles and processes will work at the family and marital level, and even in international relations.

All these principles, values and beliefs lead naturally to the outcome of empowerment. You do not have to seek for empowerment. It becomes the natural outcome of right relationships: seeing each other as equal, understanding and valuing every human being.

People learn to need others and grow into the fullness of Christ (Ephesians 4:11-13) through the equipping of the saints, bringing us into complete maturity. Right relationships lead to maturity and unity, which produces empowerment and transformation.

Dallas

Pastor Zan Holmes decided to believe in me. I was experiencing rejection and a lot of battles after the news article in 1996. Pastor Holmes understood the dynamics of power. When he asked me to partner with St. Luke on a revitalization of the Owenwood Neighborhood where the church was located, almost immediately, the resistance I was experiencing stopped.

Because Pastor Holmes had empowered me, I was released in a new way to empower others. As a result, the diverse partnerships organized by DLF came together and amazing changes took place. In just a few years, the Owenwood Neighborhood was a totally different community.

With a theology of equality that empowered each part of God's body to do its work, tangible results were multiplied throughout the city.

Nigeria

Dr. Emmanuel Nwachukwu gave the following exhortation on the idea of empowerment and how that affects what IB is doing in Nigeria.

> IB taught us about sustainability. You don't keep giving them fish. You teach them how to fish. Which is why we're doing Imani Leadership Institute, and why we're doing vocational training; getting people to stand up on their own. It doesn't matter how much profit you make, even if it is only 20 Naira, it adds to the GDP of your country. It's positive, and people get respected. People will not view themselves as poor anymore. And people get motivated to make a contribution. That's what development is all about.
>
> Empowerment [is] understanding that God has not just sent us to win souls, but to disciple them. The souls must be taught what it takes to stand on their own, to be able to replicate what somebody else did in them in all their lives. So, when we get empowered, that means that what we are doing can get passed from generation to generation. Dr. Kathy will not be here forever. We ourselves will not be here forever. Maybe the test of the work of what you have done for God is what will happen fifty years from today. Who are we handing this work over to? Who are we empowering to continue with what we now believe?

Through the IB network of partners in Nigeria, we have been able to launch numerous initiatives. The TEC (Transformational Engagement Center) in Badagry has vocational training year round, a primary school and houses the eye surgery clinic. A solar energy school operates in Ketu and holds classes in Badagry.

The Imani Leadership Institute (ILI) trains and empowers the next generation of leaders in using the BRIDGE Model to transform society through the church. A football league (soccer), led by one of our ILI students, operates male and female programs. The female league, now with over 300 young women involved, was the first of its kind in Badagry.

As Imani Bridges, we see our main customer as church leaders. We work toward empowering local leaders who will be the change agents. It has been incredibly rewarding to see the unified leadership, not just at the national level among the bishops in the Fellowship, but also, the unified leadership that is emerging in Badagry. It has been a long journey, but I believe empowerment will come naturally if the rest of the model is followed.

> "The best relationship is one where your love for each other is greater than your need for each other."
> — H. JACKSON BROWN, JR.

> "Nobody stands taller than those willing to stand corrected."
> — WILLIAM SAFIRE

There are lots of failed solar energy projects in Africa because people go into it untrained. They could do things, but they don't understand the science behind it. So, in Imani Bridges, we are training people who understand how to do it, and who can do these things effectively.

– Tony Nwachukwu, Solar Engineer for Imani Solar Academy

All these examples from Dallas and Nigeria have shown that whether starting from the top or bottom, the BRIDGE framework can be implemented and effective. Voice of Hope was more grassroots, started from a place of poverty, identifying with, and living among the poor. Dallas Leadership was a hybrid as we learned how to respectfully engage leaders of color in partnerships.

In Nigeria, the work began with teaching and building community among high level church leaders, which then became embedded at the grassroots level. I taught leaders, who then taught leaders, who in turn, have caught the vision. You will always know, not just by their actions, but by their passion, whether this new belief system has become their own.

I met Dr. Kathy Dudley as our professor in 2015 while at an Executive Masters of Ministry program of the Redeemed Christian Church of God Seminary in Dallas Texas. She set the tone immediately, requesting that we all refer to her on a first name basis, which made our interaction fluid. As soon as she began to speak, I knew we shared a passion for community transformation. I spent years in Nigeria and America, working with street kids, troubled adolescents, and training others. By 2012, I was still searching for how to implement faith-based community impact. Neither my two master's degrees nor my Christian education since 1982 prepared me for this new journey. Meeting Kathy Dudley in 2015 opened my eyes. I encountered the right praxis, which is useful to explain what I had struggled to understand, allowing a new trajectory of growth in my ministry. I have since used the BRIDGE framework as a foundation to facilitate the training of thousands of missionaries from across Africa.

— Pastor Banjo Olaniyan, Pastor, RCCGNA

CHAPTER 15

Where from Here?

We've gotten this far and seen that the BRIDGE framework can work in different cultures, and either from the bottom up, or the top down, or a hybrid of the two. So now what? Where do we go from here?

The various applications of the model that need strengthening are currently spread through various locations and strata of Nigerian society, but Badagry is what we've called God's playground. It's where the church has focused on incarnating the principles as a city-wide application of the BRIDGE framework.

Badagry, the place seen as cursed, has become the place to see how to use the BRIDGE framework in action. It is now a best practice, not only for Nigeria, but others who are interested in learning.

We continue to be challenged on how to set up businesses to support our efforts in Nigeria. This is to ensure our efforts are sustainable and won't require ongoing funding from the West.

As far as economic empowerment programs, we want to further develop our solar school with the hope of expanding into other parts of Nigeria. That would be meeting an important need as discussed earlier with the challenges of electricity in Nigeria.

An example of the model spreading at a grassroots level comes from one of our fellowship partners, Eric Ighalo. He is currently working with, among other organizations, Changemakers Africa Youth Empowerment Initiative. Changemakers Africa is an organization created for the equipping and empowering of Christian young people to bring change to their society.

Recently, I came across one of Eric's Facebook posts, and it mentioned how a number of their members had been trained through Imani Solar Electrical Energy Academy and then installed solar power for a health clinic on a remote island, accessible only by boat. This clinic was the only one on an island without electricity. Women had been giving birth by candlelight with no electricity. I immediately messaged Eric to find out what had happened!

Eric replied with a long, detailed explanation of all that had gone on. I was thrilled it had all happened without my input or even my knowing. The vision has been caught.

Eric had gone to the opening of the academy in February of 2019. It was hosted by our anchor partner for the academy in Lagos. He wanted to sign up his students from Changemakers Africa who were 300 kilometers away in Benin City. However, there was an eight-month waiting list!

Eric wouldn't accept this roadblock. Eventually, they created a special class for his students. After completing the training, some of the students decided to put solar powered streetlights in the previously mentioned remote area. A company learned about their plans and decided to sponsor putting solar power in the clinic first to assist women in labor. The students completed that job and raised funds through Changemakers Africa to install the streetlights on this island also.

This is a beautiful example of the Church pooling resources, working together across denominations, profit and non-profit: all to bring societal transformation. My desire is to see this multiplied. That is the power of the BRIDGE framework — God's people working together in harmony across all sectors of society through the church.

My hope is that people will come to Badagry and other parts of Nigeria from around the world to see God's Church engaged in a way they can learn from. They can take this knowledge back to their own locations — whether in Nigeria, other parts of Africa, the U.S., or anywhere in the world. Principles can be taken from there and applied to other contexts.

We have already begun work to create curriculum and training resources for others to use. The goal is not to have Imani Bridges all over the world, but to provide available tools for distribution.

The original seventeen bishops were spurred on by what they heard take place in Dallas, TX, through Voice of Hope and Dallas Leadership Foundation. They took the examples of the BRIDGE framework from my work there and have contextualized it for their own nation and cultures. I am humbled that they asked me to steward them in this journey over the last eighteen years.

CHAPTER 16

Conclusion

I started this book with a quote from Oprah Winfrey as she reflected upon all the people that spent their lives building bridges for people like her. She realized that she is who she is because of the bridges she crossed.

Like Oprah, there have been many incredible people who believed in me and built bridges for me to cross. Dolphus Weary was a bridge. Cathie Kroeger was a bridge. Zan W. Holmes, Jr. was a bridge. Ray Bakke was a bridge. Bill Pannell was a bridge. J. Alfred Smith, Sr. was a bridge and the bishops in Nigeria were a bridge. Without them and many others, I would not be the person I am today and this story would not have been written.

But most of all, my husband, Sayres, was a bridge. God knew I would need a lifelong partner to navigate through the troubling waters of sexism, patriarchy, and a Church and society that saw women as inferior. It would take another whole book to share all the many ways I have watched him be willing to sacrifice his dreams for me.

I realized the depth of this truth recently when he was teaching the Nigerian leaders in the Imani Leadership Institute. As I listened to him tell our story, I found myself deeply moved and tears came to my eyes.

Over and over, I heard him say, "and I died." He died to wanting to go to seminary — I would be the one to go. He died to wanting to be in full-time ministry, but God asked him to go back to work to support our family when my leadership was rejected because I was a woman. He knew he had to get out of the way, so people only had the choice to work with me.

He died to being an overseas missionary and then God sent me instead. My heart was about to burst with love and gratefulness as I listened to this amazing man who had sacrificed so much for me, but I also felt guilt that I was the one who had lived his dreams.

Then I heard him say, "But each time God asked me to die, he resurrected me to something new, life changing, and beautiful. These deaths and resurrections always led me in a direction that I would come to understand was Kingdom focused, and aligned with the heart of God, as revealed in the Scriptures. Whatever short term disappointments I may have experienced were replaced with His abundant grace, and the joy of knowing I was in the will of God. That ultimately, was my true heart's desire, to be faithful, and obey His will."

Though the years, I watched as he was judged and criticized by other Christian leaders that thought he "didn't wear the pants in the family" and "was a weak man" because he was so vocal and insistent on others respecting my leadership and calling.

God brought me a lover and soulmate who would go on this life journey with me — always as equals. God built that bridge between a man and a woman and that would lay the foundation for all the other bridges he desired for us to build. Though I was only a teenager when we married, it is now forty-eight years later, and I can't imagine my life without him.

As I reflect on this journey, I am reminded of a quote by C.S. Lewis in *The Voyage of the Dawn Treader*. "Oh, Aslan," said Lucy. "Will you tell us how to get into your country from our world?"

"I shall be telling you all the time," said Aslan. "But I will not tell you how long or short the way will be; only that it lies across a river. But do not fear that, for I am the great Bridge Builder."

I pray this book inspires you to move forward courageously as a bridgebuilder. Like Aslan tells Lucy, God is telling us His way all the time, but we need to listen. Sometimes it looks like our efforts are fruitless, but we must trust God to lead the way. We do not need to fear because we are being led by the great Bridge Builder Himself.

This is my story, but also the story of numerous others along the way, on two continents, who joined me on this journey to "answer the prayer of God."

May God's Kingdom come, may His will be done on earth and may we do it together. May we be instruments of hope and peace in a world that is in desperate need. It is my prayer that God will continue to use the BRIDGE framework to help us accomplish this, as we transform communities, together.

Endnotes

1. Fadipe, Ashamu Sewanu, "Slave Trade and Western Civilisation in Badagry: A Brief History of Human Enslavement in West Africa and the New World." 2010, SIR T Production, Lagos, p.9.

2. https://www.informationng.com/2017/04/strange-flame-fire-razed-mystery-tree-badagry-burned-17-hours.html (accessed July 16, 2019).

3. Cathy Meeks, *I Want Somebody to Know My Name* (Nashville: Thomas Nelson Publishers, 1978), 28.

Acknowledgments

Ephesians 2:9 says, "For we are God's handiwork, created in Christ Jesus to do good works, which God prepared in advance for us to do." Dr. Bill Pannell pointed out to me during my doctoral program, that the Greek word for handiwork is poiesis which means "to make." It is also the root word for poem. I believe we are the poetry God is writing, the masterpiece He is painting, and the beautiful song God is singing. When we allow God to live and move through us together in unity, we participate in the work of God's kingdom on earth.

That is the story of *Bridges: Transforming Communities Together* — God moving through His beautiful body around the globe to answer His prayer — that we would walk in love and oneness. I want to acknowledge all those I have encountered on my journey who were brave enough to move beyond the inconveniences of individualism and enter the too often uncharted waters of collaboration and self-sacrifice. You will discover many of those voices throughout this book.

However, there are a few that deserve special recognition for helping me get these stories and principles into print. I especially want to recognize my husband, Sayres Dudley. You will see his fingerprints on every page. I owe an enormous debt of gratitude to Dr. Karissa Glanville who worked tirelessly interviewing and transcribing the testimonies of numerous Nigerian and American partners. She also greatly assisted me in developing the first draft. Mona Lisa Morris, my friend and graphic designer, you know me better than most. Thank you for this beautiful book cover, the splendid graphics in the copy, and even the name of this book.

I also want to thank Dr. Sherri Lewis my editor and Dr. Mary McCracken for proofreading the manuscript. I am grateful to Susan Shankin and Precocity Press for her excellent work on design and interior layout and for working with me to bring this project to completion.

Lastly, I am forever grateful to the Lord Jesus Christ, who touched my life with His grace and love and gave me the privilege to be called by His name and to serve Him with my life.

About the Author

DR. KATHY HODGE DUDLEY is Founder and President of Imani Bridges (IB), founded in 2004. Between 1982 and 2002, Dr. Dudley founded and led Voice of Hope Ministries and Dallas Leadership Foundation in Dallas, TX.

She received her Doctor of Ministry from Bakke Graduate University (BGU) in 2005 and subsequently served as Africa Area Director and Professor of African Studies from 2005–2007. She later served as Director of Cross-Cultural Empowerment and Professor of Leadership and Community Development at BGU from 2010–2012.

She has received numerous awards and honors throughout her career. She authored the *Urban Youth Development Manual* and contributed to other publications.

Kathy is married to Sayres Dudley and they co-own Dudley & Associates, an executive search firm. She has two children and four grandchildren and lives in Frisco, Texas.

For more information, visit: www.DrKathyDudley.com

Voices of Bridges

www.ingramcontent.com/pod-product-compliance
Lightning Source LLC
LaVergne TN
LVHW091546070526
838199LV00024B/562/J